THE PATH OF RETURN

The Light of Parashakti

A Guide for Sacred Living

Jaya Sarada

Many words that appear in italics in this book are Sanskrit, translated informally. See the glossary for meanings of these, and any other unfamiliar words.

Important: Please note that this book is not intended to substitute for the advice of physicians or other health care providers. It offers information to help the reader cooperate with health professionals in a joint approach to achieving optimal health.

Grace Publishing
Grace Foundation
PO Box 1081
Freeland, Washington USA 98249
1-800-282-5292
www.gracefoundation.com

1. Chakras.   2. Aura.   3. Psychology.   4. Spiritual and Mental Healing.   5. Vital Force   6. Energy

ISBN 1-893037-01-0
Library of Congress number 2001088513

Cover, mandalas and chakra art by Karen Foster Wells, copyright Grace Foundation.
Cover design by Christine Shrader.
Editing and layout by Nancy Bartlett.
Path photo by Mari Bartlett.
Image and print preparation by Cynthia Fernandez.

To the omnipresent light that resides in all hearts,
the background of all creation,
the source from which we have come
and to which we will return.
May this light be the unifying force of mankind bringing love,
compassion, beauty and nonviolence to all expressions of our lives.

Gratitude and many blessings to:

The creator, divine guidance of my life, I live in gratitude of your unseen force and offer my life in service to your work.
My dearest divine mother and eternal friend, you are the guiding light of my life.
My daughters, Arielle and Alyssa, your lights shine brightly in my heart and I am so very honored for your presence in my life.
Thomas Clarke whose life I share, words can never express my gratitude.
Prema Rose, my most beloved friend and sister, your loving care, attention, editing and proofreading made this book possible.
Karen Foster Wells, my life long friend, thank you for the art for the cover, your sacred mandalas are dearly treasured and serve the purpose for which they were intended.
Shawna Smith for exquisite painting depicting *The Path of Return*, a path paved with gold and light.
Nancy Bartlett for her tolerance, patience and diligent editing and layout.
Christine Shrader, the illustrator and cover designer, Magic truly exists!
Alixe Hugret, a dear friend, thank you for your guidance with the cover.
Gayle Collins, a friend and mentor, thank you for your proofreading, editing and help with the healing manual for this book.
Jennifer Green for your assistance in designing the charts.
My sacred circle of friends.
Special thanks to Joni, Maren and Helene, for your proofreading.

ALSO BY JAYA SARADA

Trust in Yourself - Messages from the Divine

CONTENTS

THE PATH OF RETURN

The Light of Parashakti

Volume One of the Art of Sacred Living Series

The path of return is paved with
blessings of love, light,
truth and beauty.

Enjoy your journey.

INTRODUCTION

The Path of Return is an invitation to align your body, mind and emotions with the eternal light of your soul.

Through this alignment you can access the healing power of divine energies, creating optimal health and well-being in your life.

Before birth there was just silence. The desire to be arose along with the manifestation of a physical body. Our body, mind and emotions became the vehicles to experience life as a separate individual soul. Our mistaken identification is formed through our thoughts of becoming, wanting, grasping: the source of all suffering. Through taking The Path of Return to the origin of consciousness, the seeking ends and we rest in the peace and unity of our eternal essence.

The Path of Return lies before you; a journey through consciousness to your divine spirit. In this book you will explore the root causes of suffering and your deep conditioning. Through the awakening process you return to your sacred nature, which has been waiting for you throughout life.

The journey of your soul leads through the physical, mental and emotional planes to the celestial plane, the home of your true nature. The chakras, the gateways of your soul, open through the transformation process as you ascend into finer and finer vibrations of truth, wisdom, light and love. Through the union of your personality and soul you experience the sacred heart initiation.

To begin requires learning to walk lightly in the spirit of joy, free from the burdens of the past. The sacred path asks only that you have an open heart. The gentle winds of the divine are guides along the way.

The path of return leads back to the source of being. You forget what you have known about yourself through time and memory. It is the path of rebirth into your sacred nature, the eternal presence within. The path teaches the development of compassion for all beings encountered along the way, forgiveness of those who trespassed along your path and forgiveness of yourself for trespassing on the paths of others. It asks you to release all discordant energies developed through separation from your divine source.

The path of return is a journey to the realization of your self. You will find the divine love needed to overcome all obstacles along your way. The great spirit guide brings the gifts of wisdom, discernment and vigilance as you make the difficult passage back to your soul's home. You will learn to see through the illusions of life to the truth and find peace that is unaffected by outward changes.

The journey begins with you!

A JOURNEY IN
CONSCIOUS AWAKENING

The Mandala of Consciousness
Mistaken Identity
The Journey of the Soul

In early stages the disciple identifies the Soul with the physical self, next duality comes and there is a distinguishing between the higher self and form self. As one progresses along the path, doubt, uncertainty appears and then one wonders how to be of service. The personality then begins to fade in the background and a light on the path appears. One then becomes a channel of soul energies, expansion of consciousness into what has always been present, one's eternal being-ness.

Aart Jurrannse

Chapter One

THE MANDALA OF CONSCIOUSNESS

We descend from the heaven realm, creating a physical body as the vehicle to understand our divine nature. The journey of return begins with learning to be firmly planted on this earth and trust the unfolding process of life. The path to the heart of our soul is unique for each of us, but the destination is the same for all; the return to the source of our divine origin.

Our energetic make up is woven of many levels of consciousness, beginning with the physical plane and evolving to the formless plane of the divine. *The Path of Return–The Light of Parashakti* is the study of how we can access divine energies to bring healing, balance and alignment to our threefold being – the body, mind and soul. In order to access these higher planes of the healing light, it is essential to turn within and discover our true essence. By understanding our sacred nature, we can turn to this eternal presence, the source of all light and healing. This presence teaches us to honor all of our being and begin to treat the body as a temple, the mind and emotions as expressions of our true nature and our soul as deeply sacred.

The path of return takes us on a journey from physical manifestation through our emotional and mental natures, gradually coming home to the temple of our soul. Each plane of consciousness that we evolve through is a vehicle for understanding greater aspects of our being.

Most of us spend a lifetime developing a strong sense of self, which constitutes the personality aspects of our human nature. Our personality is the integrated expression of our body, mind and emotions, which originates from the first three planes of consciousness: physical/etheric, astral and mental. Our physical/etheric is our body of prana and life force, our astral body is the seat of our desires and emotions and the mental body is the source of abstract thinking and the concrete mind. Our sense of who we are originates from the identification with our personality nature. This temporary aspect of our being is based on time, memory and thought. We often miss the opportunity in life's precious moments to investigate further into the unknown essence of our being. When we look past the temporary nature of our personality into our higher planes of consciousness, we open the doors to our eternal soul.

Throughout our lives we are challenged to master ourselves in this suffering world, to develop inner strength, courage and perseverance. There is a profound yearning to know more about ourselves, to deepen our understanding of our purpose as human beings. Through investigation into the nature of our true self, we can observe that the personality aspects of our being (what we know through time and memory) can no longer define who we are. We initiate the mastery process by turning within and listening to our soul. We can then begin to take a stand for our true nature and quit believing our thoughts, emotions and memories are our only identity. As we deepen our awareness of our divine reality, we journey into the fourth plane; the home of our soul. The door will open to our soul when we dissolve our personality into the healing light of the sacred heart, the source of all love and oneness.

Through surrender and grace, we ascend into planes of greater and greater consciousness beyond time and form. These are the spiritual planes of the atmic, monadic and divine (adi), representing the source of joy, spiritual will and freedom; the gifts of our life, our soul's birthright. We are on the path of return to our sacred home, found in the sanctuary of our heart; a place of deep peace and silence where our vital force flows, nourishing the body, mind and emotions. Through the transformation of the lower vehicles we ascend from the temporary nature of life into the ever-present beingness of our true reality.

Identifying with the changing appearances of life and our separate sense of self with all of its sorrows, losses, pleasures and pains, we often close our hearts to our sacred soul. We then become prisoners of past memories and captives of worry about the future. As this painful habit of identification continues through the passing years of life, our vital force is chipped away leaving little or no energy to be in the moment.

This work encourages a different view, one of empowering our being, honoring life's experiences and evolving through its lessons. Then by the process of deep surrender, we find the freedom to live life anew. A new way of being will open through this freedom, where we will live in constant remembrance of the eternal force within us that is present throughout all of life's changes.

With the deep understanding that our eternal reality is not subject to experiences of time, we can observe the changing appearances of life with detachment. This simple practice renews our sacred energy, keeping it vital for the ever-unfolding journey of life.

When we awaken to the sacred presence within, our compassion comes alive to the inherent suffering in this temporary world of old age, sickness and death. Our radiant heart then guides us to live our most precious moments on behalf of the eternal force that is behind all of life. Each day becomes another opportunity to look within our heart and discover the essence of love, the vital current of our being. The divine action of turning toward our everlasting, true nature opens the door to freedom. Through this celestial doorway, we embark on *The Path of Return*.

REFLECTIVE PAUSE

To live fully is to honor each sacred moment with
complete freedom from the past.

THE PERSONALITY

Planes of rebirth and physical expression

The Physical or Etheric Plane

Made up of channels through which vital energy flows and sensations are experienced, this subtle body includes the pranic sheath and the etheric double and is related to the sense of hearing. Corresponds to the sexual organs, adrenal glands and root and navel chakras. This is the body of prana and the source of our physical fire.

The Astral or Emotional Plane

The energy surrounding the physical body which is subject to the five senses. Thought, doubt, exhilaration, depression and delusion are experienced in this body. Related to the sense of touch. Corresponds to the pancreas, the external form of the solar plexus chakra. This is the body of desires, emotions and sensations.

The Mental Plane or Intellectual Sheath

Controls and guides the mind, the ego and the sense of self. Related to the sense of sight. Corresponds to the thymus gland. This is the body of the higher and lower mental which bridges our soul and personality.

THE TEMPLE OF THE SOUL

Planes of the formless expression of the divine

The Atmic Plane or Buddhic Consciousness

The causal or seed body. Just as the seed contains within it an exact blueprint of the plant it will produce, the causal body stores the subtle impressions of the divine in the form of karma. These impressions control the formation and growth of the other two bodies and determine every aspect of the next birth. The causal body is the home of intuition and divine consciousness, the source of love. It corresponds to the throat chakra and externalizes as the thyroid gland.

The Monadic Plane

Manifests as the energy of transcendence. Related to the third eye center and externalized as the pituitary gland, this plane is the source of joy.

The Divine Plane

Corresponds to the knowledge of being, the formless plane of divine consciousness, the source of divine will and ultimate freedom. The plane is related to the development of the crown chakra and externalizes as the pineal gland.

We forget we are soul actors
We become lost in the stage
We become identified with costumes
We lose sight of the story
We forget our true home
We sever our connection with our source

Chapter Two

MISTAKEN IDENTITY

Our lifetime offers a wonderful opportunity to realize our true sacred nature and to learn to love and care about our self as an integrated system of body, mind and soul. This requires purification of the personality nature of our being, where our emotional body is stilled and our mental body is in balance and inspired from our Buddhic nature; the source of our pure consciousness.

Our vital energy is essential for our well-being. When it is flowing freely we experience an optimal level of health and wholeness. During times of stress, our vital force is affected and therefore we experience a depletion of energy on some level. Depending on the origin of the stress, it may affect us physically, emotionally, mentally or spiritually. When stress is unresolved we identify with thoughts, emotions and patterns that stem from the past. Given the art of seeing, we can use our awareness as a tool to look and see the root causes of our suffering, whether it be organic, emotional, mental or spiritual. Through our gifts of awareness we apply the healing power of love, to correct problems from the root cause.

The *leelas* (Sanskrit for divine plays) of our lives display our most interesting legend. Our life can be looked at as a story, where the stage and the scenes are constantly changing and we play a part accordingly. Although our temporary nature and personal selves are the characters in our stories, the profound message of life is that our real eternal nature is always witnessing the play. When we believe that our true essence is the temporary character in the story, we suffer according to the act as it plays out. As the scenes change in the drama of our life, our identification with the impermanent nature of life often creates sorrow and suffering. The key to balance and harmony with our threefold being is to know throughout all changing scenery that the background of the play is our true essence, the sacred current behind our life. Our sacred being is eternal and untouched by all experiences of the world. Paying more attention to our true unchanging essence, we begin to disengage from these temporary roles and enjoy lightness and detachment. This lightness allows for peace and calmness and we no longer take the changing nature of life so seriously. Fostering and nurturing the power of our true self, we bring a much-needed love, the source of all healing, to our life.

Through detachment from what is temporary and the roles we play in the changing scenes of life, we learn the art of emptying out – bringing the necessary space to our life to free our vital energy. This requires a sincere interest in letting past impressions and habits of wrong identification go. When we unify with the greater aspect of our true nature we begin a process of expanding our consciousness to a new level of freedom. This freedom leads us to surrender limited ways of being that create contraction and personal suffering.

When identified with our small sense of self, our life seems to manifest in limitations. When we identify with our greater being, our awareness expands to our eternal nature, the bonds of time and memory fall away and we walk the path to freedom.

Throughout the history of mankind, we have failed to understand the meaning of existence and our sacred nature. Because of our mistaken identity we have developed a complicated web structure around our life force, causing traumatic impressions and memories to be held within the physical, emotional and mental aspects of our being. The holding of past impressions in our system prohibits our vital force from renewing and rebirthing its natural energy. When we return to the simplicity of our being without a relationship to the past we experience a new freedom in our life.

Our sacred life force must flow without hindrance throughout the aura. To experience our true potential we must release our personal history and our relationship to the past. Becoming current we are born anew, and born anew, we revitalize our core and align our beings with the eternal divine force of life. The art of letting go of the past is the beginning of healing. In this surrendering process, realignment with our divine energies takes place. A unified energy system with a healthy mind, healthy body and healthy emotions, brings a sense of wholeness and renewed vitality and we experience the miracle of perfected life.

The simple truth is that within all human beings is a sacred heart, the source of true and long-lasting healing. When we turn to this sacred heart, the essence of love, truth, forgiveness, perfection and compassion becomes our divine medicine. As we take the path of return we open our inner channel to divine energies or the light of parashakti. This sacred energy has the ability to heal any imbalances of the body, mind and emotions.

In the study of *The Path of Return - The Light of Parashakti*, we will observe how each plane of consciousness is vital to the integration and functioning of our whole self. We will learn to detect the source of our imbalances and their root causes. We will also learn what the soul asks us to do before true and long-lasting healing can take place. We will discover the intention of the soul, what our energetic system needs to come into balance and where to apply the healing power of love.

The first three planes of consciousness are the physical, emotional and mental bodies, which form our personality. Our vital force, or prana, is the energetic web that holds the planes together and is contained within the etheric body. Our true Christ-like nature may be realized in the fourth or Buddhic plane. This plane of consciousness holds the current of selfless love, the beginning of the path of return to our Father's house. Through building the bridge between the personality and soul we ascend into the plane of divine love, becoming a truly human being.

Following is a brief explanation of how imbalances begin in the physical, emotional, mental and spiritual planes of consciousness. In-depth study of these subtle planes is contained in the chapters on etheric, emotional and mental planes.

On the physical plane, illness is generally a result of stress on some level; not paying attention to warning signs such as fatigue, loss of energy, depression and pain. When we listen to the body, we are able to detect imbalances before they manifest as illness. We can learn to sense our bodies' internal messages and follow what the body is requiring for its sustenance. When the body speaks to us in the form of pain or discomfort, we become its most cherished caretaker. Honoring its messages and yielding to its direction brings balance to all aspects of our being. Through this listening we learn to apply the healing force of love to our life, observing the root cause of the imbalance. For this we must be honest about our thinking habits, our emotional expressions and our connection with nature and the divine in life. If we are diligent we can usually trace a physical symptom back to an emotional experience or a time of negative thinking. We can also observe when our life is calling for communion with nature and the silence of our divine self. The living question, "Who am I?" takes us into the reality that we are not our body, but must cherish it as a vehicle for our journey home.

On the astral plane, imbalances usually begin during periods of emotional stress when we are not allowing emotions to flow through and out of the body. When anger, for example, is suppressed time and time again, it usually turns into depression and often leads to a weakened system. Anger that is expressed too strongly breaks down the internal organs and opens the body to disease and disharmony. Anger is merely a call to speak our truth at the appropriate moment with ease and honesty. Anger, when rooted in fear is a reflection of our disharmony with divine energies and can be transcended through increasing the vibration of love in our lives.

Emotions are a gift to understand others and ourselves. From them we learn the art of listening to the voice of the heart. This requires energy and freedom from past emotions that color our experience of life in the now. When emotions build up from the past they become lodged in the aura, waiting for new experiences to assist in their release. Because of these past emotions it becomes difficult to live in the now. To be well emotionally, we must learn to let go and die to the past, releasing all past trauma. When letting go of the past we must consciously surrender our attachment to memory, give all to the sacred fire of life and begin to fully live in the present.

On the mental plane, imbalances begin when the mind is not used constructively. The mind is like a piece of clay and needs to be molded and refined to be the most useful tool. When the mind is not directed properly, it is open to negative thinking habits that can result in illness and disharmony. The mind, when quiet, can be an instrument of beauty, perceiving spiritual truths of the universe. Through the quiet mind we have access to our higher nature which holds the healing light of love, wisdom and compassion.

The mind, when allowed to run unguided, expresses thoughts of a lower nature, which directs the emotional level to feelings of anger, greed, desire, attachment, fear, envy and so forth. When the mind is used as a witnessing tool, it can be of great service on our journey, assisting us to stay centered, still and well-balanced throughout life's changes. In this way the mind is mastered and unwanted thoughts no longer dictate our actions. We can learn to train the mind away from paying attention to outward thinking through turning it in to the silence of the heart.

On the spiritual plane, the core cause of imbalance is our lack of faith in the divine in life – a loss of our inner self by identifying with the outer world. As soon as we identify with our true nature of pure consciousness, we no longer are affected by the display of opposites found in this changing world. We remain in balance, focusing our attention on sustaining the sacred energy that resides within our heart.

During our lifetime, we can either let life's experiences defeat us or honor them as sacred pointers to our true reality. We can observe how life is a movement of grace that is guiding us on the path of return to our true nature, often stripping away our false existence. In this honoring we strengthen, expand and grow as we meet the challenges and tests that life presents. We become a co-creator with life and see that in all things are hidden blessings, pointing in the direction of self-understanding and self-realization. We are shown, through our daily life, where we need to apply the sacred and healing force of love, surrendering our personal will to this most humbling force, yielding to its direction and lessons in self-mastery.

We can learn to be spiritual warriors, skilled in energetically warding off negative forces and tendencies from our lower nature. Then it is possible to guard and cherish our sacred energy as a most precious jewel. This jewel of consciousness within is our dearest companion as it guides us to a life of peace, wellness, divinity and great beauty.

The essence of life is pure grace that leads us to understand the gifts of outer challenges and tests. When the gifts or lessons can be extracted from life's experiences, then our vital energy flows through our being and is not retained in memories that are unresolved. Seeing the grace of life and learning the lessons of the soul allow us to live in the moment. In this freedom, our being has the vitality to face the challenges of life without the encumbrance of the past. Lessons are learned by surrendering to our divine nature and realizing the purpose of this life is to evolve in the love and truth of pure consciousness.

Our divine self is the background of our life. It witnesses our temporary nature riding the waves of pleasure and pain and all aspects of duality. The background remains silent, watchful and ever present as the temporary nature of life weaves a story of endless change. In healing the body, mind and emotions, we turn away from changing appearances and meet the eternal nature of our sacred heart. This meeting redirects us to love, peace, compassion and communion with our divine creator.

THE DIVINE MEETING

The divine meeting can take place only when we become still, so still that we hear the whisper of our soul residing in the temple of our heart. The art of listening brings us into the presence of our innermost self in its truest perfection. Once we know our perfection we will reflect it in all aspects of our life, for life is a mirror of consciousness. We are, in our true essence, pure and perfect. When the blocks to our pure consciousness are removed, the light and radiance of our being is revealed. This radiance displays a new picture of ourselves as one with the infinite beauty of the divine.

Our suffering is caused by our identification with ourselves as the characters in our stories creating an unforgiving life of suffering, guilt and remorse. In meeting our true essence we have the opportunity to stop the identification with the stories of the past, bring ourselves current and align with a presence of being.

But the essence of our being has receded into the background while the separate individual self has come to the foreground. The personality self is in control, manipulating life according to its self-centered programming. We must reverse this order of control to begin to know God and our divine self. This means that the chattering ego self, the belief in the importance of our thoughts and desires must recede into the background and merge with the source of divine consciousness.

The path of return is open to all who turn to their eternal, divine nature. The test of life is to make this turn to our true nature. From there, grace leads the way, a simple way. We must shift our identification from our temporary nature to our eternal nature that resides in the silence of our heart. The light within the heart clears away the darkness of misidentification. When we take the path of return, all separateness merges into the heart of our true nature. We are home and are no longer lost in the wilderness of our temporary personality. This recognition brings the security of the divine, where all questions are answered and all doubt is removed.

The healing force within each of us can uncover that which is vital, perfect and full of goodness. For this to occur we must learn to surrender and let go of the past and the identification with pain and pleasure. We must truthfully see the areas of our life that have been created from the web of mistaken identification. We must look at the way these webs have brought suffering to our life and contributed to the suffering of mankind. From this seeing, the deep compassion and the love of our heart awakens, releasing all things that are not of the highest good.

Learning to live in this moment where our vital force is accessible we see the gifts of the past, gather strength from its stories and use its lessons to deepen the goodness of our human nature. But we each must see clearly that we are, in reality, not a separate personal self.

REFLECTIVE PAUSE

We are eternal beings and our essence is untouched
by all experiences in time. Meeting the vital force within
occurs naturally as we bring our energy into the
moment and focus our attention on the eternal.

THE PATH OF RETURN

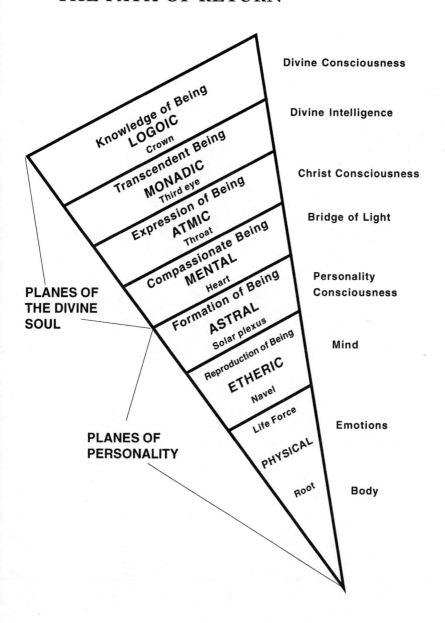

Divine Consciousness

Divine Intelligence

Christ Consciousness

Bridge of Light

Personality
Consciousness

Mind

Emotions

Body

Knowledge of Being
LOGOIC
Crown

Transcendent Being
MONADIC
Third eye

Expression of Being
ATMIC
Throat

Compassionate Being
MENTAL
Heart

Formation of Being
ASTRAL
Solar plexus

Reproduction of Being
ETHERIC
Navel

Life Force
PHYSICAL
Root

**PLANES OF
THE DIVINE
SOUL**

**PLANES OF
PERSONALITY**

Whatever you can do, or dream you can, begin it.
Boldness has genius, power and magic in it.
Begin it now.

                                        Goethe

Chapter Three

THE JOURNEY OF THE SOUL

Inward, is the word he utters to me who wished to know the path. Inward, inward is the path (of return) for everyone, the path is inward.

Sri Ramana Maharshi

The journey of the soul begins with manifestation and ends with un-manifestation. Harmony of form and formlessness creates the essence of wholeness, where the healing light of love flows unrestricted through body, mind and soul.

The word aura comes from the Greek word, *avra*, meaning breeze. The aura is the sum total of the seven planes of human and divine nature. The spheres of energy surrounding the physical spiral progressively outward forming strong energy fields. Seven planes in the solar system relate to the seven planes of the human being. We begin on the path of return when we realize our physical body is a vehicle to fully embrace our creative life force. Our inner being uses this vehicle to explore not only what it is to be human, but also what it is to be divine. Our physical and personality expressions come from the first four planes of consciousness, the physical, etheric, astral and mental. As we ascend past the limitations of our personal identity, we open the door to the true nature of our celestial body. Beyond our human comprehension are the formless planes of the heaven realms, the atmic, monadic and adi.

THE SEVEN PLANES AND THEIR INFLUENCE

Level	Plane	Correspondence
1	Physical	The physical plane relates to the element earth, corresponds to the root chakra, the endocrine and adrenal glands with the energy of grounding.
2	Etheric	The etheric plane relates to water, corresponds to the navel chakra, energy of vitality and physical expression. The navel chakra externalizes in the endocrine system as the gonads in males and the ovaries in females.
3	Astral	The astral or emotional plane relates to fire, corresponds to the solar plexus, energy of fire or will. The solar plexus chakra externalizes in the endocrine system as the pancreas.
4	Mental	The mental plane relates to air, corresponds to the heart center, energy of love and compassion. The heart center externalizes in the endocrine system as the thymus gland.
5	Causal	The causal plane relates to ether, corresponds to the throat chakra, energy of truth in creative expression. The throat chakra externalizes in the endocrine system as the thyroid gland.
6	Monadic	The monadic plane relates to the sixth sense, corresponds to the third eye chakra, knowing, intuition and union of dualities. The third eye chakra externalizes in the endocrine system as the pituitary gland.
7	Adi	The divine plane relates to pure consciousness, corresponds to the crown chakra, integration of all, and surrender. The crown chakra externalizes in the endocrine system as the pineal gland.

REFLECTIVE PAUSE
*Through the integration and union of our human nature and our
divine nature we evolve into our highest potential.*

Nature has woven into our being many strands of vital force
that connect us with the higher planes of consciousness. As integrated beings, our physical body is the mansion of our life; our etheric
body is the electricity and current, holding the mansion together
through its vital, pranic force. The meridians, chakras and *nadis* are
the pathways through which our vital force flows. The meridians bring
energy to our internal system; the chakras bring energy to our psychological and spiritual system; the nadis weave together, intercon-
necting us with the source of our life force. When the electrical currents of our energetic pathways are unobstructed and flowing, our
mansion remains strong. When the current is weakened or energy
is blocked somewhere in the system the physical is open to disease. Through understanding that all is energy, we create clear energy flows throughout our system, allowing for optimal health and
well-being.

Our vital energy is the key to the health of our body, mind and
spirit. When we learn to measure our energies we can detect imbalances before they manifest as illness. Through energy healing we
become adept at rebalancing our circuits, recharging our system
and keeping our life energy intact. When our life force flows without
impediment, we experience alignment and balance. When it is
blocked somewhere in our subtle anatomy, we experience constriction and a depletion of energy on some level. Through early detec-
tion of the etheric we have the ability to keep our energy flowing.

As all aspects of our makeup affect each other, we are truly
integrated beings. When observing the physical plane of manifestation we see how impressions of our emotional nature affect the way
we feel and respond to life. We often hold impressions from the
past in our subconscious and therefore, respond emotionally based
on past experiences. This identification that we hold prohibits us
from being fresh and current with life. To be well emotionally we

must learn to let the past go and allow our feelings to have space and newness. The nature of our sacred life force is self correcting. Our innate intelligence guides us to be empty of the past, to open to the moment and truly experience the art of being. The emotional and mental planes are interrelated and together create the way we respond and think about our lives.

Our mental energy has two aspects; the lower mental based on emotions from the past and unresolved life issues and the higher mental based on inspiration from our spiritual nature that is free from impressions from the past. The lower mental is the aspect of ourselves that expresses concrete thinking based on our separate sense of self. The lower mental plane thrives on thoughts of an un-healthy nature, thoughts that feed the emotional body, creating emo-tional and mental illness and disharmony. When thoughts are based on desire, greed, envy, hate and other forms of violence, we call forth emotions to fuel them for action. Actions based on these ill emotions and thoughts create pain and suffering in our lives and the lives of others. When thought is observed and not acted upon, we learn the art of witnessing. We begin to see thoughts like clouds in our mind, drifting in many different forms and expressions. Just let-ting them flow through our mind is the beginning of healing the mental level. We learn to discern thoughts that pertain to the order and clarity of life and thoughts that are identified with personal desire and self-centered motives.

Our higher mental body is evolved through the inner work of letting go of the identification with our personal self. The personal self is confined to thought that is based on time, memory and condi-tioning. Our sense of separation comes from this conditioning. When there is a meeting with the sacred that is found in the heart, a deep surrender of the individual self occurs. This letting go brings a new level of intelligence into our lives, one of inspiration, intuition and clear seeing without a past.

The personal self may be defined through the sum total of all experiences based on the past, held in the cellular memory of our body, mind and emotions. Thoughts, when fueled by emotions, create a disconnected sense of self, a veil of ignorance most difficult to overcome. Through the identification process we are conditioned to believe in our passing thoughts and emotions as our true self.

The personality nature relates to the physical world through sense impressions. These impressions form the personality's definition of reality. When we realize our true nature is found through the formless, eternal aspects of life, we are no longer blinded by this misidentification and we take the path of return to our true self.

Through the interrelationship of the emotional and mental planes we can observe the root cause of imbalance and disharmony. The connection between the planes of consciousness provides an important key to discovering our true nature. Our journey takes us through the consciousness of our limited self to ascend into our higher nature. We then expand to our divine potential, the source of all love and light.

When identified only with the form aspects of life, which exclude the planes of our higher consciousness, our human experiences become reflections of this limitation. These experiences usually reflect that of worldly materialism, identification with the body, our roles and status in life and so forth. Believing these aspects are our true reality we fail to move into the greater realm of our divine nature. In reality we are ever-evolving beings on a journey of unlimited mystery.

When we journey beyond the temporary nature that is bound in identification with our lower impulses in thought and emotions, we open the door into the higher mental plane, the home of our sacred heart. We begin to quiet our thoughts and emotions, surrender the obstacles to our essential nature and seek to understand the mystery of our life through listening, honoring and being.

THE BRIDGE BETWEEN PERSONALITY
AND DIVINE CONSCIOUSNESS

We are given a most sacred heart where the wisdom of the universe can be found. Turning our thoughts and emotions to the quiet of our sacred heart, we move past the limitation of our personality nature. Through our evolving awareness of our divine nature we experience life in deeper and deeper ways. Our spiritual practice widens to include the care necessary for our humanness and the care necessary for our divinity and we learn to live a life of balance and harmony with our whole being. To live in balance is to walk the earth with a sense of being grounded; honoring the gift of life, while at the same time knowing we are on the path of return to the sanctuary of our soul.

When the mind turns in to the stillness of the heart and rests there, all sense of separation ends. The spiritual heart of our being dissolves all divisions that have been formed through outward identification. Awareness of our spiritual nature leads us to observe that our separation is a product of thought and emotions sustained only by the mind. The ego's purpose is to uphold its identity apart from its source, living a life of separation on the never-ending wheel of cause and effect. In reality this sense of self is the illusory web that blinds most humans. When this is seen as a mirage, the veils fall away and freedom is ours.

When the mind is trained to live within the quiet of the heart, there is peace, joy and unity with life. The mind that follows thoughts and emotions, creating the never-ending stories of suffering, has not come to the peace of the sacred heart. It is considered the "Monkey Mind," a slave to the ego, jumping from one thought and emotion to the next. To break the habit of the mind that identifies with thoughts and emotions as being our truth, we must train the mind to rest, to sink deep into the true reality of the heart, where the undercurrent of love is found.

As we come to the realization that our true self is not bound by anything we naturally turn to the eternal essence of life. In our awakening, we begin to know life as an expression of one sacred source.

This expanded awareness produces a unity with all of creation. We see the undercurrent of life as the unfolding power of love that is giving, allowing, opening, being and surrendering. In our willingness to expand, life becomes a spiritual gift leading us to greater and greater aspects of our sacred self.

The nature of our pure consciousness has three aspects:

light - seeing things as they are

love - seeing others as they are

energy - service to all.

When our true nature is unobstructed by the veil of the personal self, we become radiant beings with love, light and energy.

The revelation of our real nature begins when awareness moves beyond the impermanence of the known into the unknown mystery of our celestial being. Our true nature lives in freedom, beyond the limits of the body, mind and emotions. When we cease to identify with what is known through time and memory, the miracle of life unfolds before us.

REFLECTIVE PAUSE

*When we allow for this occurrence, there is a diving
into the eternal current of life.*

THE ANATOMY OF THE SOUL

The Etheric Body - The Source of our Vitality
The Astral Body - The Source of our Emotions
The Mental Body - The Source of our Thoughts
The Causal Plane - The Source of our Intuition

Chapter Four

THE ETHERIC BODY

THE SOURCE OF OUR VITALITY

Many occult sciences agree that everything in nature has an atmosphere or electromagnetic field surrounding it. This energy duplicates the physical and is called the etheric body; a fluid-like substance visible as a band of light around the physical, protecting and shielding it from outside negative influences. The etheric underlies and interpenetrates every atom, cell and molecule of the physical body. Its energies move in fine channels closely related to the nervous system, nourishing the entire body with prana, the life force. The etheric body is the framework on which the physical is built and through which the body is fed.

Prana is the sum total of the life energy of the universe. It is the inflow of energy from the sun, stimulating and energizing the etheric body in rhythm with the universal heartbeat. The etheric receives prana in several ways. Solar prana, emanates from the sun and enters the physical through the head and shoulders. Energy is passed to the spleen and distributed first to the root chakra and then to all other chakras. When the etheric is in good working order, the prana circulates freely, keeping the physical form organized and energized. The etheric body also receives planetary prana from the planets. The planets absorb solar prana, circulate it through the planetary etheric body and then transmit it to the physical planet where it is cast off as radiation.

Our etheric body is affected by the way we take in and absorb

THE FUNCTIONS OF THE ETHERIC BODY

Receiver of Prana - Prana or life force is received from the sun and then absorbed by the etheric body via certain centers found in the upper part of the body and then directed downward to the etheric spleen. This is the main center for reception of prana; the other two being the center between the shoulder blades and slightly above the diaphragm forming an etheric pranic triangle.

Assimilator of Prana - Prana is absorbed, assimilated and distributed throughout the physical body. The etheric transmits energy to all parts of the etheric vehicle; as the spleen assimilates the energy it then passes it on to the chakras and various organs.

Transmitter of Prana - The physical/etheric system receives prana from cosmic sources via the three centers: the spleen, shoulder blades and the point above the solar plexus. After the prana is received it is distributed to the rest of the body.

Protective Functioning of the Etheric - The fluid-like energy of the etheric creates a sheath or web that divides the astral from the physical. This web-like energy circulates through the body into the spleen and then the chakras. Here it animates and vitalizes all physical organs, protects the physical body from disease and absorbs and distributes prana in a balanced way throughout the system.

prana. Imbalances occur when the three centers that receive prana are not in good working order, when the spinal column is out of alignment, or when the spleen is unbalanced.

When prana or life force enters via the spleen chakra, the excess energy is discharged through the pores of the skin to form the health aura - a luminous force field around the body. The degree of health of the physical body depends on the amount of prana that reaches the aura.

The etheric is called the health aura because it emanates strong or weak streams of vital force according to the well-being of the individual. The electric energy of the health aura is seen as a luminous gray or violet mist that duplicates the physical body about a quarter of an inch from the skin. Another word for the health aura is ectoplasm, which is a term used to describe the etheric energy that constitutes the state between energy and matter. It determines our health as well as provides a protective force field which shields the body from negative influences. When the energy is strong the etheric body is smooth with streams of light vertical from the physical body. When there is an imbalance in the system the rays will show signs of weakening and droop, reducing our ability to fight illness. The physical will then show signs of stress.

The etheric is the mold for the physical body. After conception the etheric body is formed; then the physical counterpart or duplicate is created from this blueprint. The etheric body forms a barrier between physical and astral planes. Only through the development of consciousness can the two energies communicate or interchange. Consciousness expands through meditation and concentration.

Through energy healing we may learn to detect imbalances in the health aura, determine where it is weakened or depleted and then balance disturbances by correcting the flow.

The personality is reflected within the aura as it gives and receives impressions from the soul. An example of how the aura is perceived may be seen in social contacts when a magnetic personality, which has a bright, attractive glow is seen influencing all those with whom the person comes in contact.

Throughout the aura, bands of energy overlap each other to form the whole aura. The etheric body constitutes the inner aura. The second part, shaped around the body in an egg-like form, is the emotional body; the third band of energy, shaped like a heart, is the mental body. The mental body is open at the top to let vibrations (impressions on the physical) of a higher nature pour through.

The mental body provides a force field protecting the subtle bodies from imbalances and disease. The mental body is where we make clear decisions regarding our health and healing journey. This is the energy plane, where our affirmations, the spoken word, our choices and healing thoughts are effectively used. All these play an important part in our healing and wellness process.

The next subtle body, the astral, interpenetrates the etheric. Between the etheric and the astral is a protective sheath that prevents astral or emotional energy from overwhelming the etheric. Injury to this shield can be very dangerous and usually comes from emotional shock. Dark forces, which penetrate the etheric through violence, anger or fear, tear the etheric/astral sheath and open one to illness. Drugs and alcohol create tears in the sheath and send the poisons to the astral plane.

Since the etheric is closely related to the astral body, it is permeated at all times with emotions from the astral body which directly affect the physical state. When stress and emotional trauma enter our life, damage first appears in the etheric, weakening the physical body and making it vulnerable to illness. The astral body in turn is greatly affected by our thought patterns from the mental body. The mind also has a strong effect on the etheric body. Depending on the level of thinking (either negative or positive) it will be reflected in the emotions, then the etheric, then the physical body.

Patterns of imbalance in the mental body stem from negative, non-factual thinking. With every wrong thought, we create a disturbance in the etheric body and the life force of our system. When we strive for clear thoughts we transmit the healing energy of these positive thoughts to the physical body via the spleen. Emotional purification also plays an important part, eliminating all harmful and negative emotions, filling our life with love and peace. Focusing on expanding the higher centers purifies the etheric and charges our system with vitality. Deepening our awareness shows us how emotions and thoughts play an intricate part in understanding the key to our good health and well-being.

In looking at the causes of illness and suffering we must take into account the totality of our being and how each part is deeply interconnected. There are many ways to purify and enhance the well-being of our body, emotions, mind and spirit. When these planes communicate, integrate and create an upward mobility of consciousness, we experience a great vitality.

Through the etheric we are an integral part of the entire kingdom of nature. A force of energy surrounds every living thing; rays emanate from the aura's core just as solar rays emanate from the sun. Within this energy body are thousands of pathways of life forces, called *nadis*, meaning motion or vibration; threads of life that underlie every part of the body. Nadis are webs of energy that flow to the physical from the universal life force and the outer world: the sun, the planets and the seven cosmic rays. The soul uses these channels to pour its life energy into the system.

The etheric body is a network of these fine energy channels, interlaced by an energy stream which links the physical and astral body. This is called the *silver cord*. Through an intricate weaving of subtle energies within the etheric, the silver cord connects all the vital centers keeping us grounded through the many lessons and experiences of life. Another name for the silver cord is the *sutratma*. This is the life thread that incarnates at the beginning of a lifetime. The pearls of human existence, containing the seeds for future births are strung along this cord. The sutratma is the central channel where the free flow of life force travels on the energetic path of return connecting our personal self to our divine spirit.

A threefold thread runs along the spinal channel: the *ida, pingala and sushumna*, forming the path of life. The ida follows the left side of the spine and is the white or lunar channel that is related to the love and wisdom aspect of our being. The pingala is located on the right of the spine and is the dark or solar nadi related to matter and intelligence. The sushumna is located within the spinal column and is related to the father or "will aspect" of love. The *sushumna* is the most important *nadi*, the channel through which our soul energy travels. It gradually widens through evolution and through conscious awakening, the *bridge of light* or *antahkarana* forms. This conscious awakening is the outcome of fusion between our personality and soul, opening a direct pathway to divine consciousness. The pathways of the ida, pingala and sushumna relate to three centers: the solar plexus which is related to the impulse of desire in life, creative urges and the physical sun; the heart center which is related to the impulse of love and divine expression and the head center which is related to the will to live.

The bridge of light is built step by step as one evolves on the path of return, linking the entire being into an integrated expression of divine consciousness. This process is called continuity of consciousness where the human soul awakens as an entity on the physical plane, using the physical body, emotional body and mental body as vehicles of soul expression.

The physical and etheric planes are where the life force begins. The physical/etheric plane represents a sense of being-ness, an acceptance of our life in the body and trust in life's process. Having this awareness in daily consciousness brings the physical plane into a healthy balance of living in the now.

The next plane of consciousness is the astral, the seat of desires, emotions, feelings and sentience. Through the journey on the path of return we must learn to integrate the emotional plane with the etheric, creating an unblocked flow of feelings corresponding with our heart and soul. When we accept our emotions, embrace our feelings and release them, we heal the emotional body. This also creates health and vitality in the physical/etheric body. Through the upward striving of our being we learn to transcend the astral plane into alignment with our higher purpose, which opens the gateway of our heart.

The plane that is interwoven with and connected to the astral

COMMUNICATION OF THE SOUL
WITH THE PERSONALITY

The Silver Cord (thread of life) infuses the physical with the life force through the blood stream. This sacred cord unifies the subtle bodies and is anchored in the heart center. The silver cord makes contact with the soul through the evolution to the mental body.

The Creative Thread is the cord that links up with the center at the base of the spine. The creative thread is responsible for the development of the personality and when evolved it expresses and is anchored in the throat center.

The Consciousness Thread or Antahkarana, which means bridge, is the inner organ or mind and is anchored in the pineal gland of the crown center.

plane is the mental plane, a band of energy slightly beyond the emotional field. The mental plane can create thoughts to enhance and uplift our life, or thoughts of a negative and constricting nature. Strength of mind can overcome all challenges. The thought processes (good or bad) filter down from the mental plane into the emotional plane to create feelings. These feelings then affect the physical plane. Depending on the nature of the thought the physical plane expresses either balance or imbalance. We can change the direction of our life simply by changing thought patterns. Learning the art of meditation, focusing on positive, life-affirming thoughts and aspiring toward higher values, are all tools of well-being. When we see that our life's journey can be described as a spiral of upward energy, surging to higher realms, then all parts of our life reflect that upward spiral. When our life spirals down to negative ways of being, with actions based on dark thoughts and life styles that support a downward way of being, we suffer immensely.

THE ETHERIC CHAKRAS
GATEWAY OF OUR LIFE FORCE

Throughout the etheric, channels of energy create a web around the physical. Where these lines cross they form centers, or wheels of energy, called *chakras*. Chakras are the controlling stations of the life force, provide major points of contact with the outside world and are potent receivers of impressions from the higher realms.

There are seven major chakras in the etheric body. Each plays a part in nourishing and sustaining the nervous system, organs and endocrine glands. The etheric chakras are different from the emotional and mental chakras, they specifically function to keep the physical balanced and healthy. These chakras are essential to the life of the etheric and glow according to the development and health of the individual. The etheric chakras influence the vitality of the whole system. They distribute prana throughout the etheric body, which then brings the life force to the physical. The chakras also function as communicators or transmitters from one plane of consciousness, linked to the various bodies.

The first three chakras make up the aspects of the personality. Related to earth, water and fire they are associated with physical survival. The next three chakras relate to air, light and an integration of all elements, making up the spiritual aspect of our being.

The first center, located at the base of the spine, is called the root center or *muladhara*, which means support at the root. With four petals of fiery red and orange tinged with gold and yellow, this chakra is a whirling vortex of energy flowing into the reproductive organs. This center, related to the earth element, energizes the sexual organs and externalizes as adrenal glands, governing the spine and kidneys. *Kundalini*, the serpent fire, resides here.

The second etheric center is the navel. Called *swadhisthana*, meaning sweetness, this chakra is located at the midpoint of the sacrum, externalizes as the gonads and ovaries and governs the reproductive system.

The navel chakra is related to the water element and has vermilion petals. Through this whirling center the life force circulates with the purpose of reproduction of being and the physical creative force. Energies come into the body through the spleen and then are distributed to the remaining chakras.

The solar plexus chakra or *manipura* is related to the astral plane and affects the digestive system. This third center corresponds to the liver, kidneys and large intestine and is associated with feelings and emotions. Because this is the power center of the physical body, where instincts and survival play an important role, it is easily exhausted. Predominantly yellow, this lotus has ten petals. The solar plexus center is related to fire.

The heart center or *anahata*, meaning un-struck, is located behind the heart in the dorsal spine. Its twelve petals are a golden green color for healing or a rose pink for divine love. It externalizes as the thymus and governs the heart, circulation and the blood. The energy of the heart corresponds to the compassion and love of the Buddha or Christ. The heart center is related to the life prana and the element of air.

The throat center or *visuddha*, meaning purification, has sixteen petals of whirling blue, light blue and other colored energies. Located at the lower cervical spine in the area of the throat, it governs the vocal chords, bronchia, lungs and digestive tract and externalizes as the thyroid and parathyroid glands. Called the chakra of miracles for its connection with the powers of life and its ability to express intelligence through the spoken word. The throat chakra is related to the element of sound.

The third eye center or *ajna*, meaning to know or perceive, is located between the eyebrows on the forehead. It governs the eyes, teeth, sinuses, lower brain and the stem of the brain. The ajna chakra has two main petals of intense white with hues of purplish blue and violet. Related to the anterior and posterior pituitary glands and etheric sight the ajna is the command center of our being. When aligned with the soul it brings clear thinking and vision, intuition and truth. This chakra is related to the element of light, where visualization becomes the gift of seeing in manifestation. Opening this center merges the dual nature so life is unified and whole.

The crown center or *sahashara*, meaning thousand petaled lotus, is located on the crown of the head. It governs the brain and nervous system and externalizes as the pineal gland. Through union and harmony of the heart and crown centers love, will and intelligence are balanced, opening the channel for the soul. The heart and mind, when aligned with the soul express in love and wisdom the foundation for harmlessness.

The chakras represent the transformational journey on the path of return to the source of our pure consciousness. The root center is the beginning of manifestation, our relationship to the earth where we feel a connection and purpose of life. The navel center takes us into our physical and creative energy. In the solar plexus center we experience a sense of false inner power and learn to transform our identification as a separate individual. The heart center opens us to the vibration of love and transforms the joy of being to the joy of giving. The throat center awakens as we learn the art of expressing our inner truth inspired by love and wisdom; the third eye center opens as we see beyond the duality of appearances into the oneness of manifestation. The crown center integrates all our centers into perfect harmony, connecting us with our source of pure potentiality and universal consciousness. A complete description of the chakras can be found in chapter ten, Gateways to the Soul.

The following passage by the Tibetan Master Djwal Khul depicts the Father, Son and Holy Spirit or will, love, wisdom and active intelligence when the energies of the heart, crown and throat are divinely coordinated.

"Out of the lotus in the head springs the flower of bliss, its earliest form is joy. Out of the lotus of the heart springs the flower of love, its earliest indication is wisdom. Out of the lotus of the throat emerges the flower of living forms, the earliest understanding of the Plan."

KUNDALINI SHAKTI

Kundalini is the rising or awakening of our inner *Shakti* (energy) from its latent state. Kundal means to coil, depicting a snake-like energy, which lies dormant at the base of the spine in the root chakra. Kundalini Shakti is the feminine energy of our innate power, the un-awakened aspect of our being. A powerful electric current, Kundalini Shakti moves through the chakras along the spine. It is awakened through change in consciousness as well as through spiritual exercises, dance, yoga and music.

Kundalini, although dormant in most people, has a surging force that propels us to awaken our being to merge with our source of pure consciousness. Our divine aspect or *Shiva* energy resides in the crown center and is the spirit of our nature. Shakti, residing in the root center, is the aspect of our being that relates to form and is our evolving nature. When Shakti travels upward to merge with Shiva, a union of spirit and matter creates a marriage between them. Through this union we touch unconditional love and joy.

The chakras exist in the energy body as forces of consciousness. As each one opens, the Kundalini energy is free to move upward on its journey back to its source. The path of return leads us through the graduated planes of consciousness, opening the chakras and lifting the veil to our pure consciousness.

The chakras open along the spine, one by one, through the transformation of our inner being. Our journey leads past the survival aspects of the first three centers of the personality, into the doorway of the heart. The journey becomes lighter as the ascension process takes us into the throat chakra, where the rhythms of our true nature are expressed through sound. As each chakra flowers and opens to its fullest, the journey continues to the third eye command center where we awaken to our true nature. At this point, all duality ceases and we may experience a cosmic unity. The symbol *Om* is represented here, meaning the beginning of all things and the end. The Kundalini Shakti ends its journey in the crown center, the thousand petaled lotus. The journey is complete and all experiences are integrated. Time, space and form are transcended.

When the energy opens along the passageway of the sushumna it pulls and pushes, disentangling the knots of each chakra and bringing profound transformation. The force, which surges up the spine through all the chakras, resides on all planes of consciousness.

The beauty of existence is that each and every human being has a spark of divinity veiled by the sheath of the personality. This is your true nature that has instinctive knowledge of divine presence and recognizes the truth and beauty of soul expression.
Aart Jurriannse

Chapter Five

THE ASTRAL BODY
THE SOURCE OF OUR EMOTIONS

The astral (starry) body is a moving field of energy beyond the etheric body, about eighteen to forty-eight inches into the aura. It interpenetrates the physical body and is often seen as an aura of changing colors. As emotions, feelings and passions flow and change, so do the colors and shapes of the astral body. The astral body is also called the *Sea of Emotions,* water representing emotions that are uncontrollable in nature. The biblical story of Jesus walking on the water (emotions) while rebuking the storm (mind) is an example of the kind of mastery he had over the aspects of emotions and mind that make up the lower self. The lower self creates the personality aspect of a human being. It is when we identify with the personality nature as our true self that we create suffering from this sense of separation.

When the astral body is in harmony with the soul and moral and mental development is of a high order, the aura becomes bright and luminous and extends out to eighteen inches or more. When the astral body expresses passions, emotions and desires that are out of harmony with the soul, the aura becomes dark and murky, contracting to ten to twelve inches around the physical. Highly developed beings have a large aura, showing a high degree of spiritual development and making them candidates for initiation. Initiations are gateways to the next level of spiritual development. As we evolve, the aura becomes larger and more luminous. Buddha and Christ had auras with a three-mile radius.

The astral matter is a grade finer than the physical, interpenetrating the etheric and duplicating the physical. It surrounds the physical body showing areas of congestion that come from negative thinking and ill emotions. It also reveals the condition of the physical/etheric body. The astral body acts as a bridge between the mental body and the physical/etheric body. The sheath between the astral and physical is a closely woven web of atoms which allows vibrations of a certain quality to pass through. Shields of astral protection are created to keep out emotional disturbances such as anger and hatred.

The astral body makes sensation possible, serves as a bridge between the mind and physical matter and acts as an independent vehicle of consciousness. The astral body stays connected to the physical by the silver cord.

The astral body is an aggregate of forces expressing passions, emotions, desires and sensations in consciousness. Development allows the astral to eventually align itself with the mental and become an instrument of the soul. Our test in this life is to learn to master the lower manifestations of the self, being mindful of its identification with itself as a separate entity. The astral is the vehicle for sensory experiences with the personality self in the center that experiences either pleasure or pain and other pairs of opposite emotions. The astral plane is where the pull of these dualities is most deeply felt. Therefore, it is also called the desire body or *kama* which is the combination of feelings and sensations. Impressions from daily life are recorded and stored in the astral body, creating a life of chaos and disorder from these disturbances. The traumatic memories of the past also create dysfunction and imbalances in the energy body if not healed and released. When unresolved memories are held in the energy field, life experiences are usually a reflection of these past holdings. The saying "live in the moment" is a most powerful mantra for bringing past emotional issues under control and accepting the situation as it is. Through quiet rest from emotional upheaval, a life prone to illness from astral instability can transform to mental clarity and peace.

Within the astral and lower mental body we become bound to earth by our desires. It is the *kama-manasic* state (mind mixed with emotions) that sets the conditions for future incarnations. Many stay in this realm, never evolving past self-gratification into the light of the soul. This kama-manasic state creates a web-like condition veiling our true nature. When the lower mental and astral become interwoven, some esoteric viewpoints see it as one subtle body. This veil over our true nature is difficult to overcome.

The path of return creates an avenue for understanding ourselves beyond our physical reality. The art of stillness stabilizes the astral energies and makes possible our experience of inner freedom. A freedom not affected by pain and pleasure. In this freedom, centered between opposites, our thoughts and emotions are calmed and we live in the energy of perfected life.

Stillness allows us to access our true nature which is revealed when we quiet our desire body, passions and sensations. We cross the stormy sea of the astral body through listening to the voice of our innermost heart. The heart awakens to assist us on our journey, guiding us to observe the impressions and disturbances of the astral body, without falling into them.

As expansion of consciousness moves from the limitation of the astral through the lower mental (concrete thought) into the higher mental (perception of being) we experience freedom and unconditional joy.

For most, the center of consciousness is located in the astral body where the ordinary person is enslaved by thought tainted with emotions. Average humanity is submerged in the illusions of the astral plane. The emotions of anger, worry, fear, etc. create a continuous irritation on the etheric body, which affects the physical. The corresponding chakra for this body is the solar plexus, where we often feel tired and achy from the stresses of thought and emotions. The solar plexus is related to the functioning and condition of the stomach, gall bladder, spleen, kidney and nervous system. Weakening of these vital organs leads to illnesses such as endocrine, nervous disorders, indigestion, gastric disturbances and headaches.

Our emotional nature, when not mastered, uses our deepest essence of love in the pursuit of outward gratification. When mastered, this essence of love can be turned inward to awaken the divine within our heart. The act of inward movement allows the heart to begin healing, for love of the divine is truly the love of our real essence. Desire is the outward aspect of love, the love for material gain in life. When the astral body is in alignment with the higher planes of consciousness love becomes an expression of the soul.

From the spiritual planes come the emotions of beauty, harmony, goodness, compassion, etc. From the personality plane come anger, fear, hatred, greed, power, etc. When emotions such as fear and worry are eliminated from the astral body we are able to receive impressions and guidance from the higher self.

Emotion is the reaction of a feeling that is registered by the mind and then sent to the astral body. When the emotion is pleasurable the mind remembers and binds us to the feeling. When the emotion or sensation is painful, the mind resists another such experience or runs away from any experience that resembles the past one. If we awaken to our witness consciousness, found in the silence of our heart, we can begin to observe how the mind is habitually seeking to repeat a past desire or running away from a painful remembered experience. Through observing this pattern and awakening to our true essence, healing is possible. We must only release past memories and allow life anew.

Emotional illness stems from emotional imbalances developed by uncontrolled desire, unchanneled sexual energies and fear.

The energy of fear is by far the most powerful negative force. It leads one to a downward spiral into the dark side of life. All humans and animals have an instinctive fear that protects and sustains the body in a natural survival response to threatening events. This instinctive fear is useful and needed while in a physical body. But the mind is a sponge for fear, soaking it up and waiting for past memories to trigger a release. When pain and misery are remembered and projected into the future a thought form is attached to the energy body creating a fear vibration. The saying "energy follows thought," is true. When fear is lodged in the aura it manifests situations for the release of that fear. Fear is created through the interaction of thoughts and emotions. This fear becomes a living part of daily life haunting and disturbing any possible connection with the soul. All thought is transient, changing and unreal. Observing thought and not believing it to be true is the beginning of mastering fear.

Understanding our essential, authentic self takes us to the path of return to our soul's light and initiates the mastery process over the astral vehicle. When we touch our soul's wisdom we understand and discern instinctive fears from psychological or spiritual fear, i.e. fear of death, fear of the future, of losses, fear of social status and so on. We are guided to see that we are a continuity of consciousness, an eternal being that moves through various vehicles for the purpose of evolving love in spiritual consciousness. Through this realization all fears will vanish.

REFLECTIVE PAUSE

*Return all fear to the source and allow it to dissolve
in the healing power of love.*

The astral body is the link between the physical brain and the mental plane, transmitting thoughts from the mental to the physical and sensations from the physical to the mental. The astral body, being a bridge between mind and matter, perceives sensual experiences as prana or our life force and transmits them into the physical in the form of sensation.

When action occurs in the external world it is the result of the communication from the astral body. When the mental body communicates, it transfers impressions to the astral that affect the etheric and then the physical. Mastery of emotions allows us to receive our soul's wisdom. The transmission channels of the astral must be kept clear, so it is vital to keep this body in a balanced state and to be open to communication from higher levels.

The astral body is the connection for the ebb and flow of consciousness between mind and body. Eventually we will have a free and unbroken consciousness from one vehicle to another, as strong links are created forming channels of communication. When congestion creates a lack of free play of forces from the etheric to the astral and the astral to the mental, it also creates physical imbalances.

The mind can be envisioned as the flame and our emotions as the wick. When the mind is tainted and controlled by the emotional body it creates the illusion of our separate sense of self. When the mind expands, touching into the light of the soul, it develops mastery over our limited identification. We then shift from a focus on our emotional nature to the higher mental plane and we embark on the path of return to our soul's light. Our ascension back to our source of consciousness leads us to release the hold of conditioned thought and emotion and guides us to the freedom of our true nature. When in the peace of our heart we find a presence of being, we learn to discern desires, passions and thought patterns that lead to personal suffering and to overcome them.

Our emotional nature affects our thoughts and our thoughts affect our emotional nature. Few people can think without feeling or feel without thinking. It is this interplay of mind and emotion that causes illness and suffering. When the mind is contaminated with emotions it can no longer function intelligently. We can learn to access the divine source from our higher nature, which will assist in mastering the mind and emotions. Through developing the higher mind we can direct the lower mental and astral to live in service to higher principles rather than self-centered interest and desire. This creates an avenue for the highest healing and provides the divine intervention necessary to return balance to the body, mind and emotions.

Kama (emotion) supplies the desire and passion element to our life. Manas (mind) rationalizes and adds intellectual faculties. It is within this union that levels of intelligence are created. All thoughts that are related to the personal self or our desire nature are expressed through the emotional body. Selfish thoughts stemming from the lower mental, or selfish emotions, from the emotional body lower the vibrations of the astral body. When goodness develops, its vibrations of higher matter bring light and wholeness to our life. Small steps toward this goodness far outweigh the effect of negative thoughts and emotions. Life becomes a journey of light, wisdom and love when the union of mind and emotion are expressed through the soul's guidance and mastery.

As long as the astral body is entangled with the lower mind it creates a difficult and stormy path in life. The higher mental body is connected with the source of God consciousness and works according to divine law. Through the evolution of the soul past the temporary personality state, the higher mental body expresses the qualities of discernment, divine perception and mastery. The emotional needs, wants and desires are now under the direction of the higher mind, creating a path that is less difficult and stormy.

Emotion, along with the lower mental thought processes is associated with activities of the lower self or personality. The activity of the emotions and the thought processes make up the personality. This kama-manasic state is the battleground for the fight to move upward into the level of the soul. The battle is reflected in the condition of the solar plexus, where the higher self and lower self meet. The solar plexus chakra is the physical sun of our being and must serve the purpose of mastery and self-control over the lower planes. When there is a continual battle with the personality and the soul, exhaustion and lack of vital force affect the solar plexus region along with the organs located there.

As the ascension process flows upward in consciousness, the test is to let go and surrender all effort of a personal nature. Through this surrender we are carried by the winds of grace past the stormy sea of the astral plane into our heart. When we journey into the sacred heart of our being we have a direct relationship with our inner Christ and no longer walk the path alone. There is a great expansion of consciousness and we begin to touch the essence of our unbounded consciousness and the deep peace of our true nature.

There are astral chakras located in the interior of the etheric double. They are closely related to the etheric chakras, divided by a pranic sheath or web. The energy normally passes from the astral to the physical without any problem but this web can be damaged through shocks to the astral such as sudden fright, emotional outbursts and the use of drugs and alcohol.

The base of the spine chakra, the seat of Shakti energy, is related to awakening Kundalini at an astral level. The navel chakra has to do with power, feelings, seeing and hearing on the astral level. The spleen chakra is the absorption of prana and the link to travel in the astral. The heart is the instrument to understand feelings. The throat is the power to the heart. The third eye has to do with astral perceptions and the crown is the integration of astral perceptions transforming them to the higher vibration of the mental body.

Attain to utmost emptiness
Cling single heartedly to interior peace
While all things are stirring together
I only contemplate the Return

To return to the root is to find peace
To find peace is to fulfill one's destiny
To fulfill one's destiny is to be constant
To know the constant is to know insight

Tao Te Ching, Lao Tzu

Chapter Six

THE MENTAL BODY
THE SOURCE OF OUR THOUGHTS

Mind is a thought cluster with the root "I" thought,
all other thoughts depend on it. Merge mind with the
source and stabilize it there.

Sri Ramana Maharshi

Most esoteric schools of consciousness view the astral and mental as one vehicle called the kama-manasic personality. For the sake of study we will separate them, but know that the lower mind and emotions create a web-like energy field that feeds off one another, forming one energy body.

The mental body exists slightly beyond the astral body in a heart shaped vortex of energy, with its entry point at the crown center. It can be seen as a dense mist duplicating the physical body. The energy of the mental body is constantly changing, moving in rhythm in response to thought. Good thoughts create a finer vibration and bad thoughts create a downward motion of the mental body. The mental body, when inspired from our higher or soul nature, expresses great beauty with moving iridescent light and color. Through the evolution of the intellect, the mental body becomes increasingly more radiant.

The mental body has two aspects, the higher mental and lower mental. This division is discussed in Sanskrit teachings, naming the lower mental *rupa,* meaning having form. The lower mental body expresses through the personality in the form of concrete thoughts tainted with emotions often creating a web of confusion. The average human being has not evolved past the lower nature of the mental body due to these limitations of the personality.

The higher aspect of the mental body in Sanskrit is called *arupa* meaning formlessness. This aspect of the mental plane relates to intuition, perception and inspiration from our divine source. The higher mental is connected to the formless, eternal presence that resides within our soul and is not bound to a physical body for existence. We are simply sparks of this infinite life force and the higher mental is the plane that carries us beyond time, thought, memory and form into our divine reality.

The mental body has five functions in consciousness: to serve as a vehicle for the self for concrete thinking, to express concrete thoughts through the physical body, to serve as a separate vehicle of consciousness in the mental plane, to develop the power of visualization, concentration and focus and to assimilate the results of experiences gathered in each lifetime and integrate them with the soul plane.

The lower mental expresses thoughts and emotions based on concrete knowledge of the personal self in relationship to the past. The lower mental is a vessel for the storage of memory, recording the sensations of pleasure or pain. The lower mind seeks to repeat the pleasurable or repel what is not pleasurable. Identification with our personality self is the aspect of our nature that is the greatest obstacle in our evolutionary path.

Thoughts and emotions geared to self-importance and self-preservation obstruct the flow of spiritual wisdom and impressions from the higher mental or Buddhic plane. Through this continuous activity of following thought, there is little contact with the voice of our true nature. The personality or lower self is constantly attracted by the material world, perceiving it as true reality, perpetuating the wheel of cause and effect.

The higher mental is infused with the light of our true nature where the mind is used as an instrument of the soul. Thoughts, actions and perceptions are based on the knowledge of the higher world, the love and wisdom of the heart.

When studying the kama-manasic state, the interplay between mind and emotion, we can observe how the lower mental rationalizes and intellectualizes the emotions. It is within the lower worlds of the personality that we are tossed about in the storms of a mind rooted in the search for emotional gratification.

The mind, which is the sum total of our thought patterns, has a great power over our life. Strong mental imagery and impressions of what we have experienced, or projections of what we will experience, convince and enslave us. This brings about a great apprehension and feeling of unrest in our life, for we are victims of the content of the mind with all of its trappings. The belief in the mind and its accumulation of thoughts, emotions and conditioning is one of the root causes of self-induced suffering and illness.

The mind's habit of seeking pleasurable experiences and repelling unpleasant experiences must come to an end if we are truly interested in attaining peace. When we accept *what is*, then life is lived in freedom from judgment. We find peace in the midst of the ups and downs of life's opposing forces: sadness/joy, good/bad and so forth. The mind, when outward bound, is constantly creating more webs of thought-induced suffering, attracting further experiences of personal sorrow. The mind, by turning inward, comes to rest and no longer has the power to create the path of thought-induced suffering.

THE DWELLER ON THE THRESHOLD

The mental body is formed through the accumulation of thought. The lower mental is sustained by the belief that our thoughts are real. Letting go of our ego can be the last test before we surrender our separate identity. The dweller on the threshold is the part of us that holds on for dear life as we approach our true nature. We must let go of our false identification with the personality in order to enter Buddhic consciousness. This dweller, or ego self continues to create tricks of illusion because of fear of annihilation. The threshold is the place in our being where we dissolve all fear and take the final leap into our unknown nature. In a sense it is a deep experience of opening our heart to the mysterious force of life that flows through our every cell.

Conditioned as a part of the human family we believe that our personality is our true identity. Our present identification with our personality nature is the root of suffering. Our true nature remains in the background as our personality dictates our life. It is a rare, divine action to turn within to our ever-present sacred self.

The personality is identified with form, memory and patterns of false power to sustain its separate self. Remaining separate from its source is its sole objective; this is how it maintains its power and control. Although the personality self appears to maintain its separation, the true self remains whole, untouched and infinitely a part of the greater consciousness. Through identification with our small self, we prolong suffering and create a life of unhappiness. The grace of life is that our true nature is a reflection of a greater consciousness and is always waiting, resting and being.

When we observe that the root cause of our problems comes from thoughts that take us away from the peace of our true nature, we begin to question the belief in thoughts and their effect on our daily life. Quieting the mind and devotion to our eternal presence found within the sanctuary of our hearts stop the process of thought-created suffering.

As our awareness develops, the veils created by our emotional and mental bodies, which obscure the truth of being, begin to fall. This occurs through the awakening of our true self, where we practice the path of return to the silence of our heart. All that enters our consciousness is observed as passing clouds. Through developing awareness we can stop believing in negative thought patterns and the emotional energy that goes along with them. We can see clearly that these habits of suffering are the cause of illness in our lives.

The awakened being observes habits or patterns of thought, belief and emotion that lead to personal suffering. Through this observation there is a direct facing of these tendencies that bind us to this illusion. Awareness leads the way through mastery of thought, as we take the path of return to the quiet peace of being-ness, revealed in the mind that has reached stillness. Steady, quiet contemplation makes it possible to live in the essence of our true nature; the sacred force that is the background of all of life. This receptive state of mind observes thoughts as being unreal to their source and releases them as they appear in consciousness.

The personal self solidifies its identity in thoughts and emotions that are based on past experiences. While this pattern continues, it strengthens the importance of a separate self. When we awaken to our true nature we observe how this continual pattern of maintaining a separate sense of self is the cause of our suffering and sorrow in the world. We commence our inner work by stopping belief in the activity of our self-centered mind, the accumulation of the past, thus turning inward to our eternal nature. Our true nature has never been touched by the past and holds no memory. Our being always remains the same: witnessing, watching and resting. Through becoming aware of our true nature, we learn to honor our body, mind and emotions as vehicles for realizing our sacred essence.

In Sanskrit there is a term, *asmita* which means "I am this." Asmita is a condition of the being that identifies with the physical plane and is convinced that it is the only reality. This is the limited reality of the being that identifies with thoughts, emotions and ideas to create the personality. To begin to remove this illusion we must start the process of observation by seeing that in truth we are not the thoughts we think nor the emotions we feel nor are we the content of the mind which includes our entire personal history. All that appears in our consciousness is changing and moving through like passing clouds in the sky. We are, in essence, the sky in which all of this manifestation is appearing.

Through detachment we can watch life move in duality while remaining still in the center. We witness nature, observing that nature's rhythm is always coming back to the center within, where duality turns to silence. The essence of living in detachment is learning the art of letting go and allowing each moment to be born anew.

Through this process we let go of accumulated thoughts, emotions and conditions created through time and memory. While releasing the past it becomes possible to live in the center of our being where the opposites of pleasure and pain no longer have power over us. This occurs because duality is a product of the past. Through learning to truly live in the moment we become free from the memory of what is good or bad and live in acceptance of what is.

When observing the creation of pleasure, which often leads to pain, and pain back to seeking pleasure, it can appear that our systems hold a deep biological self-correcting mechanism beyond our conscious control. When we observe this we can clearly see that from pain or personal suffering, pleasure is sought and from pleasure, pain is often the result. This is the law of cause and effect being played out in our daily physical existence, called the pleasure principle. Observing this phenomenon in our lives and the lives of others it becomes possible to assist in alleviating some of the personal suffering that is created.

The study of life leads us to the inquiry of desire rooted in thought. We see that all thought is goal or desire related, which is the source of all creation. Through the awakening process we can begin to discern thoughts that have to do with our practical life functioning and thoughts geared toward self-want. By observing the wanting state we begin to see that it is the source of all duality. When we stop wanting things we allow life to move in its own organic rhythm according to nature. By ceasing desire we can experience a new way of living, one that is founded in grace. The center within our heart is beyond pain and pleasure and its natural expression is unconditional joy.

When we see an eagle flying across the sky and leaving no trace, we see freedom. This freedom is our true nature, where life is lived in the miracle of the moment holding not a trace from the past. Recognizing who we are in truth is simply letting go of all ideas, beliefs and roles that we have formed through the belief in separateness.

The first step is to establish the intention for freedom. From this point on, life is lived according to that intention and commitment. No longer do we give way to passing thoughts of separation based on an unworthy sense of self and no longer do we give ourselves to passing emotions that lead us down the road to personal suffering. Through our purpose, created by the higher mental state in a sacred contract with our soul, we will learn to be a warrior holding steadfast to our eternal nature and living in freedom.

To review: the personality is the sum total of our body, mind and emotions formed through the accumulation of all experiences held in time and memory. The personality is the aspect of our nature that is related to survival, existence and worldly gain. When we realize that we are, in essence, pure consciousness, a witness to all things, we create a unity of being where our personality and soul become a unified whole. The soul, or spiritual self, becomes the master and the personality serves the intention set by the soul for freedom. When this divine action occurs, seeds of suffering are no longer planted.

As conscious evolution acts on the higher mental realms, we develop the insight to see the essence of life. When we journey into our Buddhic nature, our third eye center opens and we create a life of "inner vision." Action on the physical plane then arises from inward impressions of the higher world and intuition. The higher mental body, when developed, can be inspired from the soul light or causal body reflecting light down to the personality.

The path to our true nature brings many tests and obstacles. These tests are life's way of purifying and releasing the lower aspects of our nature to free us to express our higher nature. In order to overcome the lessons of the personality, we must awaken the higher mental body through the use of higher thinking faculties and discernment.

The higher mental or causal body is the "house of the soul" where we perceive through divine inspiration and intuition. To enter into this door of wisdom we must journey to the center of the heart, allowing the mind to be absorbed by its sacred force of love. This is the true meeting ground of the soul and the personality (the higher and lower self) where divine healing begins. The higher mental is found in the sacred heart, where personal love transcends to divine love and wisdom. It is through this transformation that the marriage of divine love and divine wisdom occurs, creating the awakened heart and mind.

By letting go and surrendering to the beauty of sacred being we begin the ascension process to our true Buddhic nature. We pass the difficult tests of the mind and return to our source of deep stillness. When opening the door to our true nature, we let go of all effort based on thought and self-gain. We live in the essence of surrender, compassion and humility knowing grace is the foundation from which all things come.

The path to freedom and wellness is to turn thoughts back to their source, dissolving the mind into the heart. Through this infusion of the mind into the heart, the true self emerges in all of its radiance.

LEVELS OF WAKING CONSCIOUSNESS

Subconscious mind, related to physical survival. This part of the mind is instinctive in nature and serves the intellect. The subconscious mind holds all impressions and knowledge from the past. Related to the physical and etheric planes and the root and navel chakras. The subconscious is subject to the downward pull of thoughts and emotions based on the past and personal identification and is the cause of all personal suffering. Our emotions, under the threshold of awareness live here - anger, fear, grief, shame and resentment.

Conscious mind, related to the feeling nature of the mind and the lower mental thought processes. Within the conscious mind the personal self is identified, the self-arrogating principle of a human being. When awareness develops the conscious mind relates to the world through this identity. The intellect is developed through the conscious mind and is related to the aspect of our being that uses reason as a practical tool for daily functioning.

Intuitional mind transcends reason to come to knowledge and wisdom through the path of the heart. Higher reasoning uses the facility of intuition fueled by compassion. One moves into a higher principle of thought, receiving more light from the source of pure consciousness. Through concentration and meditation the divine principle is attained.

Turiya, or fourth state of consciousness is the level of being that is pure intelligence, universal, non-dual, our truest reality. Beyond thought; it is the mind of light.

Buddha nature or divine self exists in everyone, no matter how deeply it may be covered over by greed, anger, and foolishness, or buried by their own deeds and retribution: when all defilements are removed, sooner or later it will reappear.

Wisdom of the Buddha

Chapter Seven

THE CAUSAL PLANE
THE TEMPLE OF OUR SOUL

The causal or intuitional plane extends beyond the mental body about eighteen inches, in an ovoid shape that surrounds the physical body. The energy of this body is radiant and full of color according to our development. The more evolved we become, the more luminous the colors of this energy body. The causal body is viewed as the intuitional body or celestial body because it is composed of vibrations of our truest essence. This body is our sacred auric egg, or the seed body; the cause of all manifestations in the physical world.

The causal body functions as a vehicle for the true self to express the divine law of love, wisdom and truth. The akashic records; the records of nature, are stories of our soul and are held within the causal body. They bring forth the strengths and attributes the soul has acquired through all life's experiences.

These stories are strung along the sacred thread or *sutratma*. As mentioned in earlier chapters, the sutratma, is the silver cord on which all experiences of human life are strung like pearls on a sacred cord . The causal body is where this thread begins and ends, the plane that determines all future manifestations. This thread weaves a fiber of holiness, the essence of goodness and truth, from each lifetime into our soul until we perfect ourselves as human beings.

The true self uses the pearls of existence and seeks rebirth to further the evolution of God consciousness, forming a new vehicle to refine or develop certain soul qualities and strengths. This intention is called *trishna* in Sanskrit, which means thirst for God. This is the source of our birth, the fuel for return to wholeness.

When there is a gap in our soul's development the lower planes of consciousness create experiences to strengthen and create wholeness. Throughout all births the true essence of our being remains whole and one with the source of pure consciousness.

The *antahkarana*, the energetic bridge, connects our personality with our soul. Through our inner development this bridge channels the part of us that has been awakened into the part that needs to be awakened. The antahkarana is constructed through the realization of our true nature. When we no longer identify with our temporary human nature of thought, emotions and sensations as a separate sense of self, the bridge dissolves and we become one consciousness.

The intuitive plane not only holds the answers to our life's lessons and questions, it also opens the door to our inner guide or master teacher. Through turning our attention away from the belief in our separate self, into the eternal essence of our heart, we connect with this loving guide. Our inner guide offers us assistance in the understanding and mastery of our personality nature.

When we take the path of return we find ultimate freedom and unlock our soul from all experiences in time and memory. Loosening the ties of our conditioning we are born anew into the mysteries of being. Our truest self has remained quiet and observant during our experiences. The observer has always been present through birth, childhood, old age and death. There is only one consciousness; all differences come from identification with the lower sheaths.

To open to the intuitive plane we must develop detachment from the illusionary aspect of life. Through mastery of our lower vehicles we ascend to the celestial plane, our soul's home.

Each lifetime is an opportunity to transform and transcend worldly knowledge and memory and enter divine wisdom. Our true

self, being the master of our personality, brings us back to our connection with the source of creation. When we evolve into the causal
body we bring forth the gifts of all our experiences and integrate
them into our soul's light.

There are four sheaths that create the subtle bodies or energy
fields of a human being. The first three make up the personality
aspect of our nature, the part of our being that incarnates and experiences birth and death until we awaken to our true self.

The first sheath is the physical body and is called the food
sheath. It is fed only by food.

The second sheath is related to the etheric or vital body and is
called the vitality sheath. It is fueled by prana.

The third is related to our mind and emotions and is called the
feeling sheath. It is fed only by feelings.

The first three sheaths, giving us the vitality for being, feed
our consciousness. The causal body is called the discriminating
sheath because it has the function of pure intelligence based on
intuition and soul wisdom. This level of intelligence is not affected
by the senses, but operates according to divine will and creative
power. The source of this intelligence is not the world or the senses,
nor is it based on the knowledge of the personality. This pure reason stems from the divine source.

The creative power of the soul allows all things to spring forth
by one-pointed thought, the source of all magic. It is when an idea
comes from the level of the soul and is deeply concentrated upon
that it is manifested. The higher mind expresses positive, creative
thought that comes from the source of our consciousness. When
identified with the personality, we feel bound by circumstances and
powerless to change our life or destiny. We are victims of our surroundings, conditioning and sense of false self; not realizing the
power we have to manifest life in alignment with our soul.

Through understanding that our true nature goes beyond the
limitations of the personality, we begin to see that we have the freedom to create new realities. We learn to live in the action of forgive-

ness; love is for giving, letting go of the past and creating new levels of beauty in our lives. The future becomes a living reality that can be molded and transcended to reflect our freedom of being.

In our energy field thought forms that stem from the past are held by our personality nature awaiting the opportunity for action. These thoughts can have a powerful effect on our life if we believe them to be true. They are often a result of our past conditioning and stem from a burdensome sense of unworthiness. Thoughts from the lower mind are rooted in desire and fueled by fear of loss. Discernment is the strength that comes from the intuitional plane, teaching us to observe the source of thoughts and not to follow them blindly. Through development of the higher mind we can alter the quality of our thoughts on behalf of our inner truth and align with the sacred essence of life. Thoughts transcend to inspiration and aspiration when they are in relationship to our higher mind, reflecting our intention for freedom.

While our intuitive self relates to the essence of life and its wholeness, our lower mind is constantly dealing with the fragments of life. The lower mind reacts to sensations and actions based on past experiences. Our higher mind discriminates and witnesses thoughts and emotions as not being true to our essence as a whole. This higher aspect of our mind seeks to understand causes rather than be a victim of effects.

Our path to freedom begins with inquiry into the most important question of our life, *Who am I?* Living this question, we journey to our authentic self, uncovering and releasing all false accumulations. All thoughts, ideas and conditioning of the self are released through the art of inquiry into our true nature.

REFLECTIVE PAUSE

The observer of our being is consciousness itself,
a witness to all things. In truth, we are this
consciousness, witnessing the play of our life.

The intuitive plane is the dwelling place of our true essence without the conditions of our personality. This is where spirit and matter become one, allowing our soul to further the evolution process and move beyond the limitations of human consciousness into superhuman consciousness. The pure consciousness of the soul is devoted to divine essence, whereas the lower mind is focused on details of the physical plane. Thoughts that are generated from the higher mind are expressed in principles, which have a powerful effect on our life. These principles are perceived by the soul and reflect the divine wisdom found in the spiritual heart.

The sum total of all incarnations is stored in the egoic lotus of the celestial plane, which holds the seeds for future incarnations. In each new physical manifestation, these seeds have to be sown to bring to fruition the completion of past actions. These seeds in Sanskrit are called *skandas,* which are permanent marks upon the soul that determine the conditions of the next incarnation. Skandas represent desires, impulses and obligations, which cause the being to forever stay on the wheel of cause and effect. All the errors of the personality that have had a negative effect on our being hold the germ of destruction. All seeds planted for goodness and truth live forever in our eternal being. Goodness develops through striving to think and act unselfishly.

On the path of return we gain a stronger glimpse of our source as our understanding deepens. Deepening occurs when we evolve into the causal or celestial plane where the discriminatory faculties of the mind become sharpened and attuned. Through our discrimination we tend the garden of our soul, weeding out the effects of thought and emotions from the personality vehicles. The celestial body is the temple of the divine spark called the *monad.* Love is the force and the source of this spark. The monad, the spark of divinity that awakens our heart, leads us beyond the limitations of birth to eternity. Our true essence is this divine spark - eternal, whole and untouched by disease and disharmony.

The aspects of the higher mind are discernment, clear thinking, divine perception, truth and wisdom. The heart center, as the center of higher consciousness, opens to its fullness when we ascend into the intuitive plane. The essence of our spiritual being is goodness, compassion, forgiveness, love and a life of service. When these qualities are developed they are of great spiritual benefit and far exceed the workings of a thousand years on the physical plane.

We practice the art of self-realization by honoring our divine nature through meditation, concentration and contemplation. Practice leads naturally to deeper levels of discernment, where inner vision is not clouded by lower thought patterns. The path of return becomes our life as we transcend our lower nature and open our spiritual channels. The lighted path is illumined from a divine source and grace becomes our guide. At this stage our true nature takes control and we begin to feel and act unselfishly, contributing to the evolution of humanity. Harmonizing with divine will is the work of our Buddhic nature, which creates deep and lasting goodness that is woven into our consciousness, never to be lost or dissipated.

When the causal body expands into higher consciousness the aura becomes enormous and brilliant. In a developed being, the mental body is healed by the causal body, the astral is healed by the mental and, finally, the etheric is healed by the astral.

On the intuitional plane we contact the stream of energies of the spiritual plane. We enter the realm of our soul star and move from the triangle of the personality to the triangle of spirit where we live the principles of divine will, love and wisdom.

The vehicle of the soul star takes us further on our journey home. The personality, fused with the soul, is no longer separate. We have mastered the need to experience life as a personal self. We have created our new vehicle of divine will, love and wisdom for our journey into deeper realms of cosmic manifestation.

Through conscious fusion of my personality and soul, I create unity of being. I am a soul star who radiates the divine expressions of love, light, wisdom and mastery. Om Shanti.

Soul Star

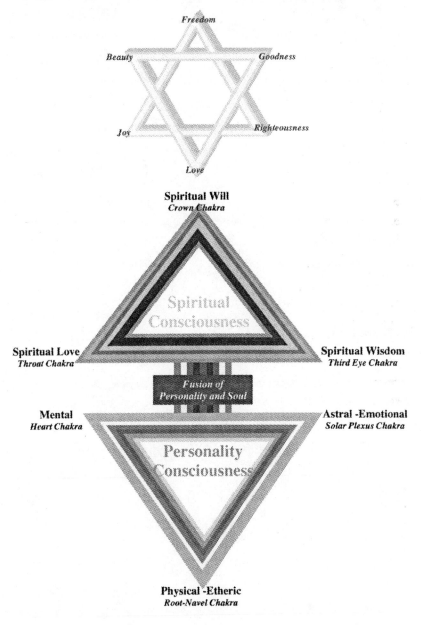

Freedom

Beauty   Goodness

Joy   Righteousness

Love

Spiritual Will
Crown Chakra

Spiritual
Consciousness

Spiritual Love   **Spiritual Wisdom**
Throat Chakra   *Third Eye Chakra*

*Fusion of
Personality and Soul*

Mental   **Astral -Emotional**
Heart Chakra   *Solar Plexus Chakra*

Personality
Consciousness

Physical -Etheric
Root-Navel Chakra

TRIANGLES OF CONSCIOUSNESS

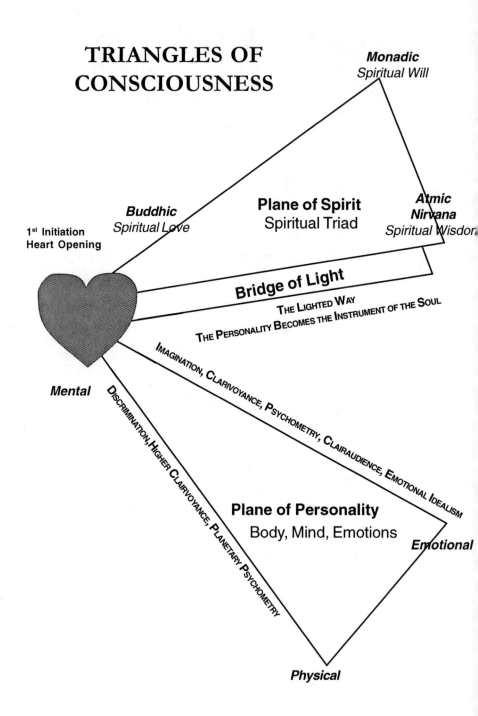

Monadic
Spiritual Will

Buddhic
Spiritual Love

Plane of Spirit
Spiritual Triad

Atmic
Nirvana
Spiritual Wisdom

1st Initiation
Heart Opening

Bridge of Light

The Lighted Way
The Personality Becomes the Instrument of the Soul

Mental

Imagination, Clairvoyance, Psychometry, Clairaudience, Emotional Idealism

Discrimination, Higher Clairvoyance, Planetary Psychometry

Plane of Personality
Body, Mind, Emotions

Emotional

Physical

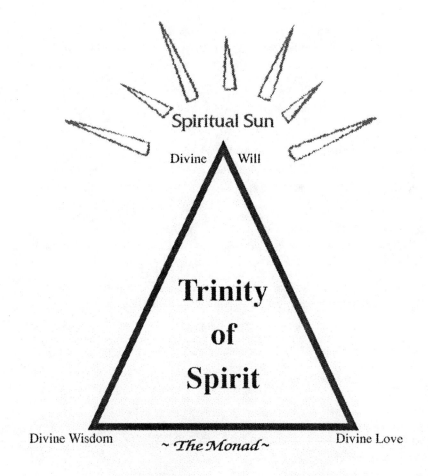

Universal Consciousness

Pure Potentiality

MEDITATION ON
THE CELESTIAL BODY

Your luminous body is your eternal nature, a radiant circle of light that surrounds your being. This is where you touch the sacred healing energy of your soul. Your vehicle of light will take you to the celestial world of the infinite.

Allow yourself to move beyond the confinements of the personality into the realm of your celestial body, which links you to the universal source of unbounded consciousness. You are, in essence, this consciousness, free from the temporary conditions of manifestation. You are formless and unrestricted by time and space. Allow your being to soar into the realm of the omnipresent force of life. In your light body all sheaths are removed and you are infinitely free. Expand into this plane of infinite beauty and celestial magnificence where you are one with the eternal.

ENERGY HEALING, TRANSFORMATION AND ALIGNMENT WITH THE SOUL

AuraTouch™
Life Force Balancing
Life Healing Techniques
Opening to the Intuitive Plane
The Parashakti Breath
Healing Mudras

Whatever be the means adopted, you must at least return to the Self, so why not abide in the Self here and now?

Sri Ramana Maharshi

Chapter Eight

LIFE FORCE BALANCING

Opening the being to God, Abide in Stillness, Life arises and passes, Birth, growth and return, A Rhythmic arc from Source to Source. In the rhythm is quietude, A tranquil submission; In the soul's submission is peace, absorption in Eternity, And so, the Great Light!

Lao Tzu

Nature is self-correcting and will naturally bring our energy system back into balance through the release, renewal and rejuvenation of our life force. All imbalances that we experience can be looked upon as sacred pointers to areas in our life where we need to apply the healing attention of love. *The Parashakti Alignment Process™* is now being applied to research in the area of body, mind healing. This tool allows us to access our higher energy and apply it to any area of our being that is in need of healing and balance.

The vital sheath (etheric body) protects our body from toxic debris of a physical, emotional or mental origin. To prevent imbalances from entering the system, this protective web around the physical must remain intact, strong and impenetrable to outside stresses. If weakened through toxins or emotional or mental stress, it opens us to negative energy that often results in a breakdown of our system.

To keep our energy being strong we must develop an awareness of our spirit nature and listen to its guidance. Our lives are very fragile and at times we weaken under outside stresses and are damaged by memories of the past. As we identify with life's passing sorrow our soul light withdraws and we loose our vitality and optimism for life. This leaves the physical body susceptible to illness, our emotional energy drained and our mind confused and unable to think clearly. To effectively create and maintain our healing light we need to learn to revitalize our soul force and call our fragmented selves back to the present moment. This occurs through breathing in vital energy, surrendering our hold on the past (whether good or bad) and reenergizing our life goals. This breathing, called the Parashakti Breath, will be described later in this section.

The physical body guides us to listen to warning signs of tiredness, fatigue or pain, the emotional body ask us to transform and release unresolved emotions, and the mental body calls us to renew our sense of self through the release of our conditioning and self-limiting belief systems. Healing the vital force requires all aspects of our energy being to be in alignment with the light of our soul.

As scientists of our energy field we can learn to detect an imbalance, find the root cause and apply the appropriate technique for true healing and alignment. When looking for the cause of an imbalance we must look to all areas of the body-mind. For example, when our physical body is experiencing symptoms; we must not only observe our physical condition but look to the emotional and mental component to discover the causative factors. The art of observing our whole being is the key to long lasting healing.

Most imbalances stem from holding frozen traumatic energies from the past. Through our developing awareness we learn to observe how our wounded past continues to be recreated in our lives. We often attract relationships that have the same factors as those that caused our wounds and co-dependent behavior patterns. These repetitions have much to teach us. It is also possible to see our life patterns manifesting through our children, our work and all aspects of our life. Our patterns can be traced back into the roots of our existence creating a map by which we can transform our lives. These roots are tied to the conditioning of our ancestors. It is possible to heal all patterns of illness and conditioning by seeing the original error in misidentification. Awareness can lead us to freedom of being and return us to the wholeness of our authentic self. When we deepen our heart's compassion and begin the healing process in our life it will radiate light to our relationships and our family and will act as preventative medicine for our future. The miracle of life is that we have the ability to instantly transform unresolved emotions from the past by seeing their core cause.

Although the past may hold stories of untold suffering, we can bring these stories into a new light and reframe them by learning what gifts they have brought to us. Like the fertile ground of our gardens, the events of our past experiences can be used beautifully to prepare our life for new and positive growth.

Our emotional nature is the watery aspect of our being, constantly changing, fluid and influenced by thought. We are called to be masters of our emotions by using the power of our higher mind to create positive, uplifting feelings. Through this mastery we have the ability to create health and well-being in our body, mind and emotions.

Our positive attitude is the key to healing on all levels; the power of our positive energy opens, expands, and reaches to our infinite possibilities. The power of our negative energy contracts, limits and is bound to the downward pull of gravity. *The Parashakti Alignment Process* creates new intentions for our being that are in alignment with our soul's light. Our soul, in its perfection, has a great healing light and will guide us to return to wholeness and peace, our natural birthright.

Healing and transformation occur when our body, mind and emotions are aligned and in agreement with our intention to be well. Through creating a divine goal or affirmation to live by, we reenergize our body, mind and emotions to be in alignment with our goal. This goal becomes the intention that the system get well, rather than allow painful suppressed memories to manifest as illness. When you find an aspiration or goal to live by, the system will support this passion and turn the energy positive, transforming all negativity. If a life goal is supported by the soul it brings a new life purpose and changes the patterns of the illness from the core of our being.

In healing our energy system we create new affirmations and visions to free our life from past sorrow. Through transformation we find a deep inner peace that can be applied to all areas of our life that need attention. When we combine the force of peace and the healing power of love and apply it to our life we see long-lasting results.

The following energy healing guide offers suggestions for healing and transforming the etheric, emotional, mental and intuitive subtle bodies. Please use this as a guideline for research, it is not intended as a substitute for medical care or advice from your primary doctor.

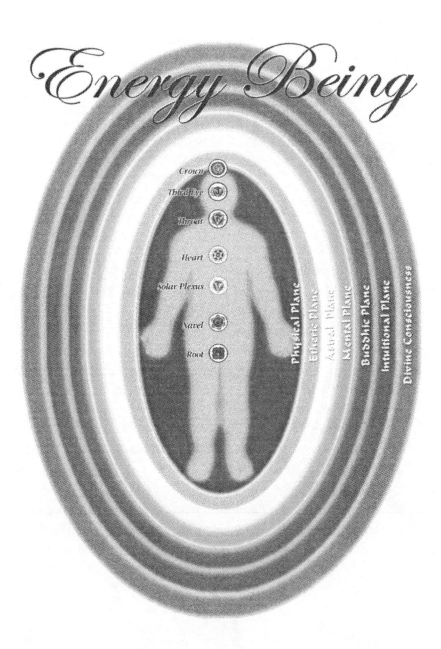

Energy Being

Crown
Third Eye
Throat
Heart
Solar Plexus
Navel
Root

Physical Plane
Etheric Plane
Astral Plane
Mental Plane
Buddhic Plane
Intuitional Plane
Divine Consciousness

LIFE HEALING TECHNIQUES

You are the light of the world. Humankind is the candle of the Lord. How important then that this light be kept trimmed and burning with the oil of pure Spirit, through the wick of peace and joy. In this way do we glorify the indwelling God.

Ernest Holmes

HEALING THE ETHERIC BODY

In the chapter on the etheric body, this energy body was described as the electromagnetic field that surrounds the physical, protecting it from outside forces. It is considered the body of prana, or vital force, as it has the job of circulating energy to the areas that need it. The first energy field that surrounds the physical, it is also the first to show signs of weakness. As discussed in the etheric chapter, signs of weakness appear as dark clouds, rips or tears in the aura, along with drooping rays. The etheric body is vital to the health of the physical and is considered the health body.

Our etheric body can be supported by a variety of methods. It responds to all physical activity, color, sound, aromatherapy, water therapy, massage, acupuncture and other energy healing modalities. The Parashakti Alignment Process offers the following suggestions to strengthen the etheric and to provide a foundation for more in-depth healing of the emotional and mental subtle bodies.

ETHERIC HEALING GUIDELINES

1. Use color therapy in your visualization. White or violet light is always beneficial to clear, stabilize and strengthen the aura.
2. Perform conscious breathing. Direct the breath to areas of the body that need healing and balance.
3. Use aromatherapy oils such as cedar, cypress, marjoram, ylang ylang, patchouli, jasmine, sandalwood in the bath or diffuser. Epsom salts in the bath cleanses the etheric.
4. Some healing stones for use in etheric healing are agate, hematite, carnelian, moonstone, tourmaline and quartz. Quartz crystals are the most sacred stones in healing. They radiate a healing, white light energy. The pointed wands make excellent healing tools, used in the fashion of a laser beam. The clear quartz acts as point a of focus for healing intention, creating links between subtle bodies and the soul.
5. Connect with nature to revitalize and rejuvenate.
6. Healing affirmations should relate to the strengthening of the root, navel and solar plexus chakras. Include those that invoke protection, grounding, stability, trust and wholeness.
7. Practice allowing your feelings to flow through you. Etheric energy is affected by the astral body. Use exercises from the astral healing section to assist etheric healing.
8. Damages to the etheric come from use of alcohol and drugs and uncontrolled emotions such as outbursts of anger. If you are subject to these, plan to reduce or eliminate them from your divine life.

When observing the imbalance of our vital force, we must learn the art of scanning our energies to see where the energy is contracting or depleted. The contraction in the system can be physical, emotional or mental causing the system to weaken. By scanning the aura, we can access the area of contraction and begin to relax the area through the healing light of parashakti. All discordant energies can be released through this healing light when we use the hands to clear, widen, stretch and expand the contracted aura.

GROUNDING AND PROTECTION EXERCISES

It is important, in working with subtle energies, to learn the art of grounding and stabilizing your energies through a vertical alignment with the earth. The earth's energies can then enter through the chakras of the feet (at the soles) and come into the body via the legs (the body's roots) into the base center (grounding center) then along the spine to the crown center. Or, energy can enter through the crown, exit through the feet and then enter the feet and exit the crown. Energy will follow its natural circular route coming in through the feet or the crown chakra, creating a vortex of healing light and protection around our system.

Grounding is a tool to use when you feel disassociated, confused and vulnerable to outside influences. It is very important to begin any healing session with a grounding exercise.

EXERCISE IN GROUNDING

Sit comfortably, spine straight, feet flat on the floor. Close your eyes, turn within and focus your attention on your lower abdomen. Breathe, allowing your inhalation to assist you in becoming fully present in your body. Find your center around the navel area. Visualize the root center and see it connected to a cord carrying your grounding energy into the earth. This grounding cord is the channel in which the energy flows deep below the earth's surface. Allow the breath to assist you in deepening awareness of the moment. Breathing out, release all thought. Breathing in, feel a sense of peace and calm. Your sacred cord links you with the source from which you came, the deep silence, origin of your being. Feel this sacred cord anchored in the earth's core, holding you in the safety of divine light. The grounding cord is connected to your foundation, giving you a sense of stability, trust and centering. Use this sacred cord anytime you need.

THE AURATOUCH™ TECHNIQUE

Valuable as a foundation for healing techniques or to end a session, AuraTouch™ uses the palm chakras to assess and heal the body.

To get started, open the palm chakras (located in the center of each palm) by rubbing your hands together, and sensing the energy. This activates the palm chakras and readies them for use.

After activating the chakras, create an energy ball and play with it for a while, this helps tune into the healing force. Hold the palms two to three inches apart and move them back and forth molding the energy field. Move your palms in and out, feeling where the energy begins and ends. Move your palms in various shapes, feeling the increase and decrease of energy. Another way to open the palm chakras is to open and close each palms twenty times, increasing the magnetic field of the hand chakras. Once in tune with your energy ball, you are ready to begin.

First scan the aura. Using your palms, follow the outline of the physical body. When you feel a change like heaviness, electricity, hot or cold, or if your hands feel magnetically drawn to an area, follow your intuition and allow your hands to receive information. After scanning, move through the aura again with brush like strokes, removing excess and negative energy. Move through the aura again with the palm chakras projecting clear, clean energy into the aura.

You can project healing energy into the affected area as long as you breathe and allow the healing light to enter your crown center. Place your palm chakra over the affected area. Use color, sound, visualizations, and crystals to enhance your work with AuraTouch™

Steps to AuraTouch™, the three R's

1. Review and scan the aura.
2. Release any energy buildup in the aura.
3. Renew and rejuvenate the aura through the use of color, sound, projections of white or healing light.

NOTE: The most important aspect of healing any energy system is channeling the energy through your body via the crown center rather than using your own personal energy.

ASTRAL OR EMOTIONAL HEALING AND ALIGNMENT

The next plane of the aura, the astral or emotional, affects the condition of the etheric. Our emotions, when unresolved, act as a slow poison that weakens our etheric energy. The state of our feeling nature not only effects our etheric and then our health, it also effects the mental plane, the source of our thoughts. Holding traumatic memories and unresolved grief, sorrow, pain or anger, slowly chips away at our vital force. Our primary organs are related to our energy body through the meridians, energy pathways along which the vital force travels.

Steps to healing the emotional body:

1. Heal repressed feelings.
2. Infuse the astral body with the healing light of the soul.
3. Bring the emotional body current through the forgiveness process and the release of the past.
4. Release subconscious programming and conditioning.
5. Release cords from binding and unforgiving relationships.

ASTRAL OR EMOTIONAL HEALING GUIDELINES

The astral body, the changing aspect of our nature, renews and balances as we release emotions from one moment to the next. This requires a mindfulness of how we are feeling, breathing in life affirming energies and releasing all residue of negativity. The practice of being in the moment allows this energy body to heal and renew its vital force. Another way to heal this energy body is to bring more joy and lightness to our life. Inspired, we see and live beauty and enjoy the simple aspects of life.

Healthy expressions such as dance, exercise, movement and singing transform old emotions into freeing ones of beauty and happiness that release the emotional body.

The use of peppermint, lemon, rosemary, cinnamon, marigold and thyme assist in clearing the emotional body. All can be used in massage, a diffuser or the bath. Certain gemstones are very effective in bringing balance to our emotional body they are: tiger eye, lapis, amber, topaz, citrine and turquoise.

EXERCISE 1: MEDITATION

Use your higher mind to transform emotions that create a lesser vibration in your life. Find a quiet space and get comfortable.

- Breathe to release tension and bring a sense of complete acceptance of your feelings.
- Accept the emotion, do not suppress or reject it.
- Allow your heart to embrace the pain and look at the root cause of your suffering. See where love needs to be applied, this love will heal all sense of pain.
- Turn within and forgive yourself and others involved.
- Breathe in the peace of your true nature.

HEALING THE EMOTIONS IN THE LOWER CHAKRAS

The lower chakras of our energy being, the root, navel and solar plexus, when untransformed keep us bound to the astral plane. This plane, the realm of cause and effect, is difficult to overcome. The astral plane represents the illusory nature of life and tricks us into believing it is real. We must learn to access the higher light of our intuitive body to assist us in discerning the real from the unreal. Use common sense in healing the astral body, realizing that it represents change, duality, pleasure and pain. All the changing expressions and events of life are products of the astral plane. Our strength comes from remaining stable throughout all changes, turning our attention to the peace and divine light of our heart. The astral body is also healed through transformation of the lower chakras: fear into love, in the root chakra; sexual energies into creative energies in the navel chakra; and desires into aspirations in the solar plexus chakra. Healing those chakras will assist in healing the astral body.

The following list of common emotions related to the lower chakras will help identify specific emotions. Negative emotions are identified with imbalance and positive emotions indicate the chakra is balanced. Breathe in to bring energy in from crown or ajna and affirm the positive emotion. Positive aspects of the emotions are good words for affirmations.

ROOT
(RELATED TO EARTH SOLID GROUNDING)

Negative	Positive
Abandoned	Cherished, loved
Anxiety	Love, trust, calm, peaceful
Constricted	Love, expanded, widened
Unworthy	Loved, honored, respected
Lack of boundaries	Love of oneself, whole
Worried	Love, trust, faith, calm
Smothered	Love, open, free flowing
Self doubt	Love, confidence, trust
Self-violence,	Self-love, self-acceptance,
Self punishment	Forgive self

NAVEL
(RELATED TO WATER, FLUIDITY, PHYSICAL EXPRESSION)

Negative	Positive
Fear	Love, trust, faith
Shame	Love, forgiveness, dignified, tolerant,
Powerlessness	Love, self aware, strong
Willful	Love flexible, open to change, cooperative
Guilt	Love, peace of mind, release the past
Embarrassed	Love, confident, passive
Unforgiving	Love, acceptance

SOLAR PLEXUS
(RELATED TO FIRE ENERGY, PURIFICATION, POWER)

Negative	Positive
Frustration	Love, peaceful, calm, relaxed
Complaining	Love, grateful, appreciative
Resentment	Love, forgiveness
Bitter	Love, forgiveness, joy
Aggressive	Love, surrender, letting go
Manipulative	Love, allowing, accepting
Victim	Love, masterful, in control, steadfast,

HEART
(RELATED TO AIR, ENERGY, REBIRTH SURRENDER)

Allow your energy being to reach for the wisdom of the throat center, express your feelings and allow them to be transformed.

Negative	Positive
Unlived joy	Love, radiant, being-ness, serene,
Humiliated	Love, honored, esteemed
Loneliness	Love, connected, secure
Betrayed	Love of self, acceptance
Greed	Love, forgiveness, peace
Sadness	Love, unselfish, fair, sharing
Isolated	Love, cheerful, grateful
Hopeless	Love, connected, united
Self-rejection	Love, trust, hope, faith
Despair	Love, self-acceptance
Unforgiveness	Love, courage, assurance
Wounded	Love, healed, whole

EXERCISES FOR HEALING THE ASTRAL BODY CHAKRAS

By healing the emotions of the lower chakras, the astral body is healed. Use the following exercises to work directly with your emotions.

EXERCISE 1: INQUIRY INTO YOUR EMOTIONS

Scan your energy body using the directions from AuraTouch™ and sense where you feel a tightness or constriction. Look into any unresolved feelings or emotions that you might be experiencing. Using the guideline above consider the chakra it is related to. On each emotional deviation ask yourself these questions: What was my original desire before this emotion? What is the core want? What is the gift of the emotion? Retrace the core desire of your emotions; see that from this desire, pain was born. Reaffirm self-love and release all need to find that love from outer sources. Next, move from the contracted or limited emotion to the expanded one, breathe in and affirm the new energy of love and light.

EXERCISE 2: RELEASING HELD EMOTIONS.

Journal regarding your emotions. Ask yourself the following questions for your journaling.

1. At what age did I first feel this?
2. Find out if the same feeling has been a pattern in your family's life, look for the root cause.
3. Ask for the gift of all unresolved emotions to be revealed.
4. Look for the gift of your life: This has taught me to be stronger in _____ .
5. Where will this lead me?
6. How does my body feel? Is this an emotion that is negative or positive in my life?
7. What is my intention for this life?
8. What is my soul's goal? Transform all held emotions through seeing their purpose and letting them go.
9. Reaffirm your freedom here and now.

EXERCISE 3: UNCHANGING ESSENCE

Either through journaling, talking with a trusted friend or on your own, answer the following questions:

1. Despite all my challenges, has something always come through that takes care of me? Give some examples.
2. Throughout all changes I have been a witness, but who is that witness? Has that witness remained safe, secure and whole? Again, give examples.
3. What do I need or want from others that I don't already have deep inside my soul?
4. What are some ways that I can remain secure and intact with clear boundaries around my energy field?

EXERCISE 4: HEALING AFFIRMATIONS FOR THE EMOTIONAL BODY

Use the following affirmations or create your own through understanding your emotional nature and life challenges. Through the use of affirmation you are able to strengthen your energy field and create a direct link with your soul. For further suggestions on affirmations see the throat chakra chapter.

1. I see myself whole and complete.
2. My wounds and memories are in reality no longer mine. They remain in the past as dust goes to dust.
3. I release all ties to my ancestral wounds, memories that are holding my energy in unworthiness.
4. I serve my purpose to be whole complete and sovereign.

EXERCISE 5. WATERFALL HEALING

Use the following meditation:

Sit in a quiet place in a comfortable position. Breathe slowly, inhaling vital energy and exhaling used and unwanted energy. Visualize an offering to your sacred self. Observe all discordant emotions that are held within your being and keeping your vital force constricted.

See yourself walking in a beautiful meadow. Ahead you see a mountain side with a big waterfall; slowly you walk into the stream and approach the waterfall. Turn within and acknowledge all unresolved emotions you are holding such as fear, shame, unworthiness, and powerlessness. Visualize yourself letting these emotions flow into an urn. Now take this urn and walk into the water. When you get to the waterfall, empty the emotional urn under the water, and then gently step under the waterfall and allow the water to enter the crown center. The water goes down the body along the legs and purifies all disharmonious thought patterns and emotions. You have been renewed, revitalized and refreshed.

EXERCISE 6: EMPOWERMENT

An empowered person is one who has gone through the effort to find his or her own truth and is consistently over time living life based on this truth. Your inner truth is the guiding force to create the life you want.

Empowerment is when your creative intelligence is aligned with your soul and your life's purpose. When you feel aligned and believe in your dreams you are a co-creator with life. Allow yourself to expand and stretch beyond your known limitations, see life as a journey into pure potential. Release control of your life and open to the greatness of your being. On an emotional level get in touch with your feelings and mold them according to your vision of life by releasing self-limiting emotions and bonds. See yourself as a warrior for your true spirit, allowing the truth of your life to guide you. Be courageous and take risks that will lead you down the road to your potential. Release all doubt and limited thought that conditions your being and holds it back in unworthiness.

Take a moment to write down your feelings regarding your empowerment. Look at areas in your life where you have given your power away. See where you have allowed yourself to be a victim because of a need or desire that took precedent over you feeling whole and sovereign. Journal your goals and positive emotions with guidelines such as commitment, trust, letting the past go, passion, magic, acceptance, change, challenges, creative response to life, discipline, decisions, truth.

EXERCISE 7: RETURN TO THE PEACE OF YOUR TRUE NATURE.

Look within to your solar plexus. Access your sense of know-ing. Relax this space and let go of strife, effort, will, and anxiety. Experience just being-ness. Notice how the mind has taken hold of the emotions here and has created a web that imprisons you. Allow your divine, healing breath to enter the solar plexus area and gently begin to let go of the struggle to become, the energy of fight or flight, the will to have life only the way you want it. Let go here and through your peace and calmness you will enter the heart center.

EXERCISE 8: FORGIVENESS

Take a journey through your life and meet all those who have touched you deeply. Look inside your heart and see the hearts of all your loved ones as one big heart of unconditional love and forgive-ness. As you walk along the path bring to your consciousness sig-nificant people in your life or someone with whom you wish to have healing and resolution. Visualize what gifts you have received from them and what you have given them. For instance, you may have received the gift of trusting in yourself. For this gift, you can now give the gift of forgiveness. Smile and say, "I forgive you." Turn to yourself and say, "I forgive myself."

Do this healing of the heart with all the beings in your life so that you may share in the gifts of spirit.

EXERCISE 9: HEALING AND REPROGRAMMING
THE SUBCONSCIOUS
AN EXPERIENCE OF FORGIVENESS AND RELEASING THE PAST

To let go of something you must first become conscious of what you are letting go. Invite what you are feeling to come very close and see it with the eyes of courage. Without going into detail you can allow the past traumas to come to the surface then transform them by infusing them with divine light and love. All negative feelings can be reprogrammed into useful attributes that you can use to increase your potential as a divine human being.

Simply look within and ask yourself:

1. From this suffering, what gift can I receive?
2. How can I use this suffering to serve my life, or to serve this sorrowful world?

Conscious Choice: Your soul is a great recycling instrument and enjoys using all experiences as ingredients to increase the vibration of light. Each lifetime is an opportunity to use karma for transformation rather than holding dormant seeds of suffering that release through unconscious expression. The seeds of your life can be cultivated to increase the beauty of your soul, reflecting your divine reality rather than your misidentified, false sense of self. Through this understanding you now have a choice to spiral upward to higher vibrations or spiral downward to denser vibrations. The choice of the upward spiral requires willingness, worthiness, expansion and devotion to the greater story of life. The choice of the downward spiral is flavored by low self worth, suffering and negative energy. The choice is yours.

If you do not consciously choose the upward spiral then your soul creates scenarios for you to experience yourself in limitation resulting in soul lessons. Through conscious awakening your life is upheld as it evolves in the love of your true nature. This magic occurs through synchronicities, divine intervention and universal support. In the truest reality you do not have a choice, all human beings are destined to return home to their divine reality, some just take longer than others.

**EXERCISE 10: JOURNALING - LIFE AFFIRMING GRATITUDE
AND AWARENESS**

1. How do you feel when you have spiritual optimism and life affirming goals?
2. How do they play out in your life?
3. What about serendipity, synchronicity? Write about the magic of your life.
4. Write how you feel when you believe in the wounds of your past, when you focus on the cup being half full.
5. What comes next from your wounded thoughts?
6. How do your wounds effect your daily reality and choices?
7. Bring a sense of gratitude in your life about everything. See all as grace. Write thoughts of gratitude down every day, use prayer to express gratitude.

**EXERCISE 11: CALLING YOUR SOUL HOME
FORGIVENESS OF THE PAST**

Allow your being to go into the quiet of your heart center. Breathe deeply and feel a sense of peace and light within. From your heart center, invoke your healing guides and ask them to gather all fragments of your being that have been scattered through time and held in traumatic memories. Use the breath to accept and visualize yourself coming back into wholeness.

You are completely present in your body. See yourself sitting enthroned in your heart; the observer of time. Your awareness leads you to heal all discordant ties from the past through forgiveness and the realization of your soul's gifts. You offer yourself in service to truth, realizing that in the light of the divine all is forgiven.

In the light of the divine only love appears, all things come from love and are returned to love. See all experience in your life as great grace or blessings in disguise; all actions have come to bless you with the fruits of learning resulting in wisdom. Send your blessing to all who have hurt you, see the ties of the past release through the transformation of pain into love. Affirm in your life the essence of gratitude, offering everything on the altar of the divine.

EXERCISE 13: STABILIZING THE ASTRAL BODY

The astral or emotional body is a whirling plane of emotions, passions and sensations, the seeds of suffering. One can stabilize this distraction through returning all outward energies to the center of the heart and stabilizing them there. See The Parashakti Breath for assistance in directing your emotional energies into the healing light of your heart. Use the peace of your true nature to infuse the outward plane of thoughts and emotions, creating calmness, mastery and peace. Practice the art of return in daily life; moment to moment bring your attention into the heart of your awareness.

The root case of trouble is the externalization
of the mind. The solution lies in our ability to find a technique that
would internalize the mind again and stabilize it in its source.

COLORS AND THEIR HEALING PROPERTIES

The astral plane is constantly changing with emotions and feelings; it has, within its realm, a wide variety of colors, thoughts and desire patterns. Colors are an important tool in the energetic healing of the emotional body.

Violet - Spiritual power, crown chakra, spiritual self
Indigo - Intuition, third eye chakra, inspired self
Blue - Inspiration, throat chakra, peaceful self
Green - Energy, heart chakra, healing self
Yellow - Wisdom, solar plexus chakra, power self
Orange - Health, navel chakra, vital self
Red - Life, root chakra, physical self

Red is considered the great energizer because of the effect it has on the physical constitution. It corresponds to the root chakra, gives vitality and creative energy to the body. Treatment with red stimulates the root chakra, releasing adrenaline into the bloodstream and can reverse sluggish conditions. Spiritually, red strengthens will power and courage.

Orange, the wisdom ray, heals the physical and cultivates inner wisdom. It controls the second chakra and assists it in assimilation, distribution and circulation of prana.

Yellow rays have magnetic qualities and are awakening, inspiring and vitally stimulating to the higher mental body. Yellow stimulates the third chakra, or solar plexus and is the color of searching for wisdom.

Green indicates harmony and balance of mind and body. It stimulates the heart chakra. It combines yellow (wisdom) and blue (truth) in a healing and rejuvenating hue.

Blue, the color of truth, perfection and devotion, is related to the throat chakra, the greatest creative center in the body. Blue brings calm and peace of mind and has a calming effect when areas of the body-mind are agitated.

Indigo indicates devotion and clear, logical thought. It is related to the ajna chakra and deals with expansion of consciousness.

Violet rays increase the effect of meditation tenfold. This color controls the crown chakra and has great inspirational effect. It is linked to the physical through the pituitary gland, which is the center of spiritual perception.

Colors and light are a reflection of the soul of the universe. The spiritual energy of the cosmic solar system is an infinite spiral of colors transmuting into spiritual substance.

MENTAL PLANE HEALING AND ALIGNMENT

The mental body is an energy band that surrounds and inter-penetrates the astral, forming a web-like field that is difficult to over come. This energy changes according to our thought forms and impressions. When healing the mental body we must look deeply at our conditioning and what we are holding onto from the past. Our mental body has two aspects, the lower and the higher. The lower is conditioned from the past and expresses itself in concrete thinking, ideas, judgments and opinions. The higher mental is inspired by our soul and expresses in the form of intuition, perception and inspiration. It is possible to bypass the limitation of the lower mental and align with our soul found in the higher planes of consciousness.

The pathway to the higher mental is through the heart chakra. Our inner work is to let go of our self-limitations and ascend into the greater aspects of our true nature. This is done through the surrender of thought, personal power, judgments and opinions and evolving into compassion, forgiveness, acceptance and the unity of the heart center. The heart and throat chakras are closely associated with the mental body.

To enhance the healing process of the mental body along with the chakras use aromatherapy oils including attar of roses, bergamot, clary sage, germanium, sage, eucalyptus, frankincense, jasmine, rosemary, lavender and sandalwood. Useful gemstones are rose quartz, tourmaline, emerald, jade, turquoise, aquamarine, lapis and opal.

The quiet mind is the key to all healing. Through the quiet mind you can reach your higher mind and expand in your consciousness to the unknown mystical being you are.

EXERCISES FOR HEALING THE MENTAL BODY

EXERCISE 1: AFFIRMATIONS TO ACCESS
YOUR TRUE NATURE OF JOY

Joy is the feeling we get when we have touched upon our true nature. Moving past the limitation of thought accesses it. It comes as grace and is not conditional upon outward circumstance. Joy is the undercurrent of our life and is found through gratitude, quiet and humility.

Use the following affirmations to remind you of the joy of your true nature. Take time to journal and meditate upon joy.

1. My joy reminds me that I am whole and complete.
2. My joy heals all sense of separation.
3. My joy rejuvenates me, purifying my being and guides me to reach my highest potential.
4. Joy allows my consciousness to embrace my limitations as well as receive the gifts of my divine reality.
5. I am pure joy, which is not conditioned upon my outside world.

EXERCISE 2: CREATE A NEW SACRED CONTRACT

In your journal create a new sacred contract; this is to be a reminder of your birthright as a divine human being. As you begin turn within to the origin of your being and allow yourself to start anew, bringing into your sacred contract all the beauty of your life.

Guidelines for creating your new sacred contract.

1. Remember that your sacred contract is free from the past.
2. All your soul's experience is transformed to goodness, empowerment and freedom. Affirm the gifts of your soul in your journaling.
3. Release the ties and cords from the past, affirm you are a sovereign being that lives in the light of your true nature.
4. Dedicate your life to truth, light, goodness and service on behalf of all suffering beings.
5. Love yourself; hold your precious being as most dear. Reframe your life to love yourself before all, for the love of yourself is the love of the divine.

EXERCISE 4: LIVING MEDITATIONS

Use these simple meditations to the path of joy several times each day:

1. Hold your true nature dear to your heart. Turn within and smile.
2. Throughout your day bring yourself into the current moment, breathe in and out affirming and reaffirming your connection with the source.
3. Love all that appears in your life as a spring from the source, letting go when you need to and holding the sacred within your heart.
4. See all with joy, embrace all with joy and ascend to the highest mountain with joy, the temple of your soul.
5. When negative thoughts such as doubt, unworthiness, low sense of self, irritation, ungratefulness, powerlessness appear in your consciousness just observe and hold steadfast to your true nature of light and beauty.
6. Practice the art of return, turning your attention back into your heart and resting in the peace of your divine nature.

CHAKRA HEALING AND ALIGNMENT

CHAKRA GUIDELINES

- Chakras record, store, regulate and communicate energy. They are transmitters and transformers of energy.
- Chakras will spin effectively when the body, mind and emotions are in balance.
- Chakras have the task of transforming lower vibrations into higher vibrations.
- They are electromagnetic control centers of the body, mind and spirit.
- If you feel sluggish physically, emotionally, mentally or spiritually you can be assured that one of your chakras is out of balance.
- Chakras receive, assimilate and transmit life energies, affecting all systems of the body, mind and emotions.
- They are gateways to our soul and higher planes of consciousness.
- The back side chakras hold records, memories of past lives and impression of the unconscious. The front side chakras hold information about our current conditions.
- Chakras are lotus-like energy centers with tubular stems that reach into our nervous system and supply the vital energy to keep the body alive.
- Chakras have counterparts on the astral, mental and spiritual planes of consciousness.
- They step energy up or down from one plane or chakra to another depending on what is needed.
- Energy flows into the center of the chakra, into the spine along the tiny pathways or nadis to the etheric body.

CHAKRAS IN RELATIONSHIP TO OUR HEALTH

1. The root chakra reflects the conditions of the lower back, spine, kidneys, adrenals, reproductive organs, small intestine, bladder, sciatica, leg pains.
2. The navel chakra reflects your source of energy. Look for signs of distress in the kidneys, adrenals, sexuality and sense of self.
3. The solar plexus shows signs of stress in the digestive process and assimilation of food as well as emotions. The solar plexus will reflect tightness due to power issues and sensing the world through feelings.
4. The heart center imbalances will show as heart weakness, life force blocks, circulation problems, general immune system problems as well as the emotional inability to love one self, or give or receive love.
5. The throat center will reflect the metabolic system as well as neck, thyroid, parathyroid, breathing and emotional issues of communication, ability to listen and hear.
6. The third eye center will reflect imbalances having to do with sight, nervous system and emotional issues of perception and understanding.
7. The crown center will affect the entire body and show signs of imbalance during any serious disease. Emotionally the crown is related to the integration of life experiences on all levels.

PAIRED CHAKRAS

A block in one chakra can affect the others. Paired chakras are root-third eye, navel-throat, and solar plexus-heart. One can be over-energized and one under. When you observe the root cause of the imbalance, use the paired chakras to guide you. The higher chakras will greatly assist the lower chakras in healing and transformation.

Root chakra imbalance shows up as lack of security. To balanced the root, open the crown center and connect with the divine.

Navel chakra imbalance shows up through misuse of sexual energies. This chakra is balanced through the throat center by creative expression as in dance, music, art, movement, theatre, writing and other artistic outlets.

Solar plexus chakra imbalances reflect issues of personal power, identification with ego and are balanced through the heart center that transforms our small self identity to our divine self, becoming truly empowered.

Crown center balances and integrates all chakras and their related physical, emotional and mental body correspondents.

CHAKRA ALIGNMENT

Visualize a beam of golden healing light entering the crown and flowing through the channel of the spine connecting all the centers with the source of consciousness to anchor in the stability of the earth. When a center feels contracted or congested, use the Parashakti Breath to expand, open and balance your chakras. Work with color, breath, nature and other healing modalities to keep your chakras aligned. (See chapter nine, the Parashakti Breath,)

BALANCING THE CHAKRAS THROUGH NATURE

Use the earth's energies to balance the chakras or simple visualizations that incorporate nature.

1. Root Center – Lotus position sitting on earth, any connection with the earth will balance the root as well as assist you in grounding your energies.
2. Navel Center – Ocean, waterfalls, streams, lakes, ponds and all watery aspects of nature.
3. Solar Plexus Center – Sun, fire, desert, heat, all warming aspects of nature.
4. Heart Center – Connection with all green aspects of nature.
5. Throat Center- Healing through connection with all blue aspects of nature, such as water, skies, etc.
6. Third eye – Healing through stargazing and night skies.
7. Crown – Healing through climbing to high places, mountains.

SPINAL BALANCING THROUGH THE CHAKRAS

The chakras play an intricate role in the alignment of the spine. Use the following reference guide to observe the condition of your spine in relationship to the chakras.

a. 4th cervical vertebra - root

b. 1st lumbar vertebra - navel, spleen

c. 8th thoracic vertebra - solar plexus, adrenals

d. 1st thoracic vertebra - heart, thymus

e. 3rd cervical vertebra - throat, thyroid

f. 1st cervical vertebra - brow, pituitary

g. Crown of head - crown, pineal

HEALING AFFIRMATION FOR THE CHAKRAS

(to begin or end a healing session)

1. Surround yourself with a white light.
2. Ask for only the highest good to come to you in any form.
3. See a golden glow of light enter your crown center and flow through the channel along your spine, healing and protecting all parts of your being.
4. Ask the golden light to release discordant energy from your aura.
5. Breathe in a healing light and see your entire energy field solid, shielded and closed with a protective force field.
6. Affirm, "I am whole complete, true and empowered with spirit, amen."
7. Always say thank you at the end of a healing session.

OUR HEALING HANDS

Our hands are nature's way of giving us the ability to heal, comfort and direct love to areas of physical, emotional or mental pain or discomfort. The palm chakras are often portrayed in images of Christ healing.

The palm chakras are given to us for use in helping others or ourselves heal our energy. For review, we open our palm chakras by simply rubbing our hands together and sensing the energy. (See

AuraTouch™.) Create a vortex of healing energy and apply it to the chakras that need healing. Use prayer, permission, water as stated in the previous guidelines for healing.

USING WHITE LIGHT TO BALANCE DISCORDANT ENERGIES.

1. To open your palm chakras, rub your hands together. Hold them within a few inches of each other, palms facing each other and sense your energy ball.
2. Concentrate on the palm chakras. Scan the aura and observe changes in the energy field such as depression, temperature difference and where your hands are naturally drawn in, as if by a magnet or force field. This is the area you want to cleanse of excess energy. Do this throughout the aura, sweeping unwanted energy, releasing build up.
3. Flick energy away from your client, into water or the air.
4. After scanning and sweeping energy move the hands again from the head to the feet and visualize white light coming into your crown center and out your right or left hand. Apply this white light throughout the body, along the chakras and where there is any disturbance. When applying the white light, be careful to breathe and allow yourself to be an empty channel for the healing force.

CLEARING THE CHAKRAS THROUGH YOUR HEALING HANDS

1. For clearing the chakras, place your palm chakras above each chakra and move it in counterclockwise motion. This will remove static energy and clear negative build up.
2. Flick your hands after the motion to remove the energy.
3. After you clear a chakra move your hand clockwise on the chakra at least one time more than the counterclockwise movements. The number of these movements depends on how the chakras feel, listen to your intuition.

Note: The chakras are tools for transformation, We balance them through a simple clearing motion (as above), use them to gain understanding of our issues and map our healing course.

AFFIRMATIONS AND GOALS TO ASSIST IN HEALING

1. Affirmations and goals: Create divine affirmation or goals to work with a particular chakra. Use the words from the chakra charts found at the end of the chapter on that particular chakra.
2. A sample affirmation might be, 'I return my energy to its perfection through this divine healing light.'
3. In any time of healing, it is important to express gratitude and conviction that the healing has taken place. An example for this is: "I thank the healing light (angels, guides, etc.) for assistance in bringing balance and harmony to this person. All is in the light of perfection. Amen. "

CHAKRA MASTERY CHART

Crown - Mastery of all fear, leading to surrender, united and unlimited potential.

Ajna - Mastery of the mind, divine perception.

Throat - Mastery of judgments and all things false, leading to the expression of truth.

Heart - Mastery of self-centered love, leading to unconditional love, peace and understanding.

Solar Plexus - Mastery of personal will and power leading to surrender, wholeness, calmness and acceptance.

Navel - Mastery of emotions leading to change, purity and rejuvenation.

Root - Mastery of time and fear, leading to your eternal connection with life.

MAPPING THE HEALING PATH
THROUGH ENERGY EVALUATION

It is important to understand that we are multidimensional human beings and our source of imbalance can stem from one or more of our energy bodies. The study of how we integrate the energies of the body, mind and emotions is vital. To be very effective, have a thorough knowledge of the energy system and how each plane of consciousness affects the other. For example: How the emotional body affects the etheric body and the emotional is affected by the mental and the mental by the spiritual and vice versa.

Through the tools of muscle testing or pendulums we can access information regarding the health of our subtle bodies. The divine intelligence within our being contains answers to questions pertaining to all aspects of our health. We can learn to access this information regarding the condition and the healing path of our body, mind and soul.

The first step in energy diagnosis is to learn how to obtain a yes or no answer with muscle testing or a pendulum. Next, it is important to ask permission from your healing guides and the healing guides of your client to proceed with the session. Through a moment of silence, prayer or healing affirmation, invoke your healing guides.

After the healing invocation you are ready to dialogue with your client. Questions will lead to more questions, deepening your understanding of the condition that has come up for healing. A sample dialogue and questions are included in this section.

We will begin by basic clearing techniques and then energy evaluation through the use of muscle testing, following guidelines on how to use a pendulum.

PREPARING FOR ENERGY EVALUATION

1. Clearing techniques are needed in order to prepare the body for energy testing. They are simple steps to create clear circuits.
2. Begin by offering water to your client. Water will assist in clearing the electromagnetic energy fields.
3. Ask permission to test and say a healing prayer or invocation.
4. Take a moment to do a short breathing exercise, quieting the mind to become receptive to the healing light. (See chapter nine, The Parashakti Breath.)
5. Use figure eight movements around the energy field to prepare the system for the testing that follows. To clear any stagnant energy in the field, apply big sweeping figure eight motions throughout the aura. This should create a clear channel in which to proceed in the muscle testing. (See diagram for figure eight movements.)

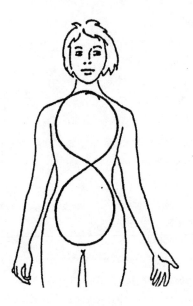

THE FIGURE EIGHT
MOTION

ENERGY TESTING PROCEDURE - MUSCLE TESTING

First discover a yes or no answer.

1. After the clearing procedures above raise your client's arm up in line with the chest and approximately 45 degrees out.

2. Remember you are not testing the strength of the individual, nor are you having a contest of your client's resistance. You are testing energy. In energy testing there is no overpowering.

3. Apply light pressure with your index finger and middle finger above the wrist bone.

4. For energy testing we apply the two second rule, the arm should lock as you apply light pressure for two seconds. If it doesn't lock, the energy is not strong in relationship to the question. This a no answer.

5. You are only checking for lock or no lock, that is the key to good muscle testing. When both people are interested in truthful answers there is no win or loose as a result of testing.

The muscle used for general testing is the pectoralis major clavicular, although many muscles can be used. We will stick with this muscle which we call the indicator muscle or IM.

Next proceed with testing

1. Begin by raising one of your client's arms up to the level of the chest and out to the side about 45 degrees.

2. Put your index and middle finger slightly above the wrist

and apply light pressure, remember the two-second rule.

3. Within two seconds the arm will lock for a yes answer.
4. The arm will not lock or it will weaken with a no answer.
5. If mushy, have the client take a few short breaths. Try again.
6. You can use the yes/no muscle test to ask questions about belief systems, such as *"I am loved"* test and if the muscle goes weak then that statement is not true for the client.
7. If it stays strong the statement is true for the person. This is helpful in recognizing counterproductive belief systems.
8. Now that you have established a base for muscle testing, continue the process to check the energies of the chakras.

ENERGY TESTING FOR THE CHAKRAS
Always have a healing journal ready before testing. Follow the steps above for preparation before a session and general testing procedures.

CHAKRA TESTING POINTS
(You do not have to touch, holding your hand above the point about two inches is sufficient.)

1. Crown center - the area of the baby's soft spot.
2. Third eye - center of head at eye level, first cervical vertebra, in-between eyebrows.
3. Throat center - base of throat, between collarbone, third cervical vertebra.
4. Heart center - center of chest.
5. Solar plexus center - center of body, below rib cage, well between the shoulder blades, eighth thoracic vertebra.
6. Navel chakra - slightly above the navel area, first lumbar vertebra, lower back.
7. Root center - In the pubic bone area, the base of spine, fourth sacral vertebra.

BEGIN TESTING

1. Check each chakra by holding your hand slightly above the chakra and testing for no or yes, which indicates a weak or strong chakra.
2. If, when testing the chakra, the indicator arm goes weak, make a note of it. (Remember the two second rule when testing.)
3. Test all the chakras and list the ones that seem weak.
4. Now go back and test the chakras, asking the question. Check for priority chakra (the primary chakra involved). This will be the chakra that needs attention first.
5. Once you've found the priority chakra, ask a sample question: "Is the source of the imbalance in the root chakra etheric, emotional or mental plane?" Note your answer.
6. When you find out in which energy field or plane the weakness is located you can proceed with balancing.

Through energy evaluation, which provides the key to long lasting healing, it is possible to discover the source of the imbalance. When you know the source, work with the healing suggestions for the etheric, emotional and mental bodies. Please see previous sections on healing techniques. For instance, if the source is emotional, you can work with the emotions of the chakra involved through dialogue and creating positive healing emotions.

THE HEALING DIALOGUE

Here are some samples of questions that can be asked when you are performing a healing dialogue. Also please refer to chart of chakra emotions in this section.

When you find through testing that the etheric body needs balancing, you will then be guided to ask questions regarding the state of physical health and vitality. These questions should be directed to nutritional concerns, overall vitality regarding meridian energy, the condition of the health body, and other healing modalities.

When the emotional body is out of balance you discover the source.

Sample questions are:

1. Do we need to look at an emotion? Refer to the emotions listed in the section on emotional healing. Use energy testing to determine the emotion involved and then the positive emotion to see if it will strengthen the emotion.
2. Do we need to look into a relationship?
3. Do we need a time frame when the condition started?
4. What does the system need to come into balance? (i.e. release of the past, letting go of a relationship, reframing a childhood trauma, working with the emotions of forgiveness, gratitude, self love).

When the mental body is out of balance, it guides us to look at our belief system and conditioning. Sample questions are:

1. Do we need to look at a belief system?
2. Check a belief pattern by asking your client to respond to statements such as "I am safe," "I am secure," or "I feel loved." Work with affirmations to bring a positive test result. See section on affirmations and healing the mental body for ideas for balancing.
3. Create a sacred dialogue that opens the system to greater levels of awareness and releasing self-limiting belief patterns.

Ask if the system is ready to create a new and positive decision based on clear vision of the primary cause of suffering.

QUESTIONS TO ASK FOR EFFECTIVE CHAKRA BALANCING

The following is a list of questions when performing a balance of the chakras through dialogue, energy testing or pendulum work.

1. Where is the imbalance located? Observe the chakra, the organs and the glands to find the source.
2. Use AuraTouch to scan the chakras. Look for areas of tension, contraction, heaviness, temperature change, etc.
3. What are the feelings located there? Investigate the emotions of the particular chakra. Related emotions are listed at the end of the chapter about each chakra.
4. Chakras can be out of balance on the etheric, emotional or

mental planes. Ask what subtle body is most affected.

5. When you discover the affected subtle body you can ask if you need to look at an emotion, a belief system, a relationship, a time frame. All of these questions will guide you to the primary source of the problem.

6. What colors do you sense around the chakra? Use color breathing to assist in your balancing procedure.

In testing you can explore emotions, relationships, time frames, childhood issues, belief system and other unresolved energies. Study the chapter on healing and transformation for guidelines. Remember to note your findings and to observe patterns that show up frequently to create long lasting healing. Always end with a positive healing affirmation, creating an avenue for your client to reach their goal of optimal health in body, mind and spirit.

ENERGY EVALUATION USING THE PENDULUM

Use this method to access the intuitive level. Pendulums are available in many new age stores or from Grace Foundation. See ordering information at the end of this book.

1. Hold the pendulum and establish your yes or no answer. The pendulum will move on one of two axes – as shown in the drawing. Usually movement along the vertical axis (up and down) is yes and horizontal movement (back and forth) is no.

2. When working with the chakras and a pendulum, place the pendulum over or in front of the chakra and observe the way it spins.

4. If it doesn't spin then the chakra could be inactive or under-energized. It may also spin in a counter clockwise manner, which indicates the energy is unbalanced. A clockwise manner should indicate the chakra is fully functioning. You can determine the differences between chakras and notice some are spinning more rapidly than others, which may require some balancing. Through breathing and affirmations you can

often bring a particular chakra back into balance.

5. You can also use the pendulum to discover the condition of a chakra by holding it over your palm chakra and asking about each of your chakras.

7. To create an energy graph use the sample and write the chakras in the slots given, put the pendulum in the middle and ask it to swing on the chakra that is unbalanced.

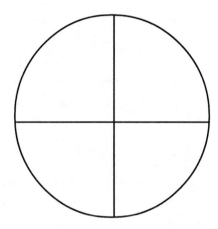

YES/ NO PENDULUM PATTERN

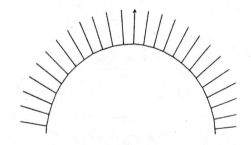

CHAKRA BALANCE PENDULUM PATTERN

The guidelines are also helpful to further evaluate your energy field through questions listed in the healing dialogue section.

OPENING TO THE INTUITIVE BODY

The Intuitive plane is the energy field that surrounds the mental. It is the home of our soul and the gateway to the higher planes of consciousness. It is our radiant body of light, full of color and energy from our truest essence. Our intuitive body is accessed through our life practice of divine love, wisdom and will. The luminous body is the holder of our soul's records and the seeds for future births. As we evolve into the intuitive plane we can access these records and begin to heal the cause of our suffering. This plane holds the answers to life's purpose, our lessons and our soul's story.

Blocks to intuition are lower emotions of fear, anger, doubt, hatred, judgment and so forth. Increases in your intuition come from love, joy, faith, devotion, service, surrender, compassion and forgiveness. Therefore, many of the exercises to heal the astral body assist us in opening to the intuitive body.

The following exercises will also assist you to open to your intuitive nature. Remember that the quiet mind is the key to healing your higher mind. Allow yourself to expand in your consciousness to the unknown mystical being that you are.

EXERCISE 1: BUILDING THE BRIDGE OF LIGHT

Your bridge of light is a gift from God constructed by going deep into your heart to meet your true nature. To begin your journey of union, create a journal of thoughts and goals for the following:

1. Develop a deep humility, releasing all sense of separation.
2. Surrender the concept that you are in control. Transcend personal power by being a channel of the divine.
3. Letting go of the limited sense of self, taking a leap of faith into your unknown mystical nature.
4. Transcend your personal will to divine will.
5. Develop a creative response to life. Trust divine teaching.
6. Experience a deep generosity through turning outward love into love of yourself and then love of others.
7. Turn within your heart and cultivate feelings of gratitude for life in appreciation of its hidden blessings. See grace in all.

EXERCISE 2: AFFIRMATION, SOUL STAR MANTRA

Through conscious fusion of my personality and soul, I create unity of being. I am a soul star radiating the divine expressions of love, light, wisdom and mastery, Om Shanti.

This simple affirmation will remind you of your work of infusing your personality with the light of your soul. Through awakening you take the path of return to your true nature of love, light and wisdom.

EXERCISE 3: MEDITATION TO OPEN TO YOUR INTUITIVE BODY

Go within and rest in the peace of your divine reality. All that comes from your divine self is an expression of beauty, free from the outward conditions of life. Your light body holds nothing and is the chalice of sacred consciousness, vibrating the joy of the creator. Release all veils that block you from ascending into your true nature and allow the winds of love to carry you home.

EXERCISE 4: CREATING A SACRED SPACE

Creating a sacred space is an avenue to consciously remember our true divine reality. The path of return is a long and arduous journey. We must find time to pause, reflect and remember who we are in truth. Stopping, waiting, observing and refueling will realign our sacred nature with our divine source. Following is a list of guidelines to create a sacred space.

1. Use the scents of lavender, frankincense, lotus and jasmine to create your sacred environment.
2. Create an altar. Use indigo, gold, orange, violet or white.
3. Say the mantra Om or other mantras (see the throat chakra section) to open your divine channel.
4. Use the crystals clear quartz, amethyst, lapis, or blue sapphire as transmitters.
5. Always have a candle burning to reflect the light of your divine consciousness.
6. Keep a vase with flowers or a bowl of water nearby.
7. Allow yourself to be quiet through meditation or silence and breathing deeply, tune in to your heart.

Wherever I shine the lamp light of Divine breath, there the difficulties of a whole world are resolved. The darkness, which the earthly sun did not remove, becomes through My Breath a bright morning.
Rumi (1,1941)

Chapter Nine

THE PARASHAKTI BREATH AND ALIGNMENT WITH THE LIGHT

Empty yourself of everything. Let the mind become still. The ten thousand things
rise and fall while the self watches their return. They grow and flourish
and then return to the source. Returning to the source is stillness,
which is the way of nature....

Lao Tsu, Tao Te Ching

Pranayama is the action of stilling the breath through deep inhalation and slow exhalation. Pranayama, pra - meaning first, na - meaning energy and ayama - meaning expansion. Parashakti is the term used throughout this book to define our divine energy. Our breath is a tool to access this energy; therefore we will name it the *Parashakti Breath*.

The Parashakti Breath can assist us in calming our thoughts, turning the mind in to our heart, the source of stillness and peace. Breathing in this way it is possible to open our channel to receive divine energy and integrate our body, mind and emotion with our soul. The descending of divine energy enters the crown center and moves through the channel along the spine, bringing light and healing to all the chakras. To the extent we can bring prana into our system, power will manifest in life as we see it.

Breathing, the essence of our life force, helps us learn about ourselves and listen to our body's rhythm. Breathing opens our reflective consciousness and helps us to see where we hold impressions from the past. The exhalation aspect of breathing can be used to let go of our past psychological holding, renewing our vital force.

The Parashakti Breath will support us in meeting our daily challenges. In deep breathing our vital force increases throughout our being, all of our senses come alive and are transformed. Our breathing gives us a spaciousness to observe where we feel heavy and where we can apply our healing light to release our unwanted burdens. Breathing takes us back to our source and brings a sense of harmony with the universal rhythm.

The Parashakti Breath is a powerful tool to realize our true nature and the divine in all of life. Seeing the illusory, temporary nature of life, we can just smile and breathe out, no longer taking things so seriously. Through the realization of our eternal being we breathe in, affirming that awareness in all the moments of our life. A slow steady breath of receiving and of letting go, will guide us to live a life of peace and beauty.

Each thought is like a bubble that appears and then disappears with no power of any sort, often distracting us from our true nature. We can observe how a thought enters our mind and stays with us when the breath contracts, as we begin the identification process with the particular thought. This contraction triggers an emotion to create the usual web that we become entangled in. Through deep breathing and observation of these waves of bondage we can exhale, allowing nothing to solidify in our mind, keeping the mind pure and free.

The Parashakti Breath opens us to spaciousness of being, where we remain in our witness consciousness, free from identification with passing states.

THE HEALING BREATH

The Parashakti Breath clears the energy channels and opens our system to a healing light that affects all aspects of our body, mind and emotions.

Breathing improperly weakens the function of almost every organ in the body. This lack of prana makes the body susceptible to chronic and acute illness and diseases of all kinds; infections, constipation, respiratory illnesses, digestive problems, ulcers, depression, sexual disorders, fatigue, headaches, poor circulation, premature aging and so on.

Many researchers believe that bad breathing habits also contribute to life threatening diseases such as cancer and heart disease. Poor breathing reduces the efficiency of the lungs, so oxygen cannot go to the cells. It retards blood flow and diminishes energy needed for normal functioning, healing and inner growth. When we learn to breathe properly we control the way we exhale, not the way we inhale.

The Parashakti Breath teaches us to exhale the old energy and inhale the new with emphasis on letting go. It is deeply relaxing and alleviates accumulated tension. Often we fail to breathe completely and then sigh a lot. This shows the need to exhale. This is nature's way of deflating the lungs when we have neglected the breathing apparatus for too long.

The Parashakti Breath is the art of breathing in our healing light. Through our concentrated exhalation we can learn to apply the light to whatever area is necessary. Once we learn to do this we can control our inner vital forces, from the dense physical body to the celestial levels of our being.

THE LIFE FORCE BREATH OF THE VITAL CENTERS

The vital centers are located along the sushumna channel and are energized by the prana they receive. Beginning in the base chakra the breath flows upward to the solar plexus and unites with the higher prana flowing downward from the crown chakra. These two forces, the apana - meaning breath flowing upward and prana - meaning breath flowing downward, form a duality of psychic energy creating a knot in the solar plexus chakra. This knot forms when we contract our breathing, holding on to a false identification. Through the process of releasing our old identifications, we begin to open the sacred heart center and this knot becomes free.

The Parashakti Breath is very important in relationship to the opening of the heart center the area of our being where we learn the art of surrender and letting go of the past. Exhaling, we let go of the past, inhaling we meet the unknown.

The chakras below the heart, feeding off the continual process of birth and death, form the personality state of our energetic makeup. Through the belief in our separate identity we create webs of thought that come from the lower self impulses, negative emotions such as; worry, fear, anger, impatience and anxiety. These webs can easily be released through the deep exhalation that teaches us to let go of our false identification and touch our eternal essence.

The seven major chakras are principle energy intake centers. The prana taken in travels along the nadis, the subtle body's nervous system. To review: the three main channels of life energy are the ida, the pingala and the sushumna. These energy pathways carry the vital force to all areas of our body, mind and emotions. These channels depend on the life force breath, to heal and balance our entire system.

The ida and pingala, corresponding to the autonomic nervous system, are responsible for the maintenance of vital force throughout our body. The sushumna is related to the central nervous system and is the channel for the Kundalini Shakti. The pingala flows along the right side of the sushumna, related to the sun. It has the yang qualities such as aggressive, logical, analytical, outer directed, rational, objective, hot, masculine, mathematical and verbal activities. The ida flows along the left side of the sushumna related to the moon, it has yin qualities such as calmness, intuitive, holistic, inner directed, emotional subjective, feminine, cool. These energy channels flow from the base chakra, weaving up the spine in a snake like manner and meet together in the third eye center. The sushumna is the pathway of the Parashakti Breath, our divine force that runs along the spine.

EMOTIONS AND THE BREATH

Our breathing habits reflect where our personal holdings are, where we contract and identify with passing appearances. When we exhale we let go and return to our natural state of stillness. When we inhale we tighten and contract and identify with a passing thought or emotion.

As the passing emotions of anger, fear, guilt and grief enter our system they are solidified by our shallow breathing. The emotions of our higher centers such as love, compassion, kindness and joy, come with exhalation and release of our small identification.

Our shallow breathing creates a vulnerability to negative emotions and our expanded breathing brings spaciousness to our experience. The breath allows us to move into the peace of our true nature and reflective consciousness. When disturbed, our emotions can be viewed as passing clouds in the sky. Our breathing assists us in remaining centered and calm. Through the quiet mind we have the option of choosing peace rather than problems or conflict, releasing our personal holdings. Our deep exhalation process gives us the tools necessary to surrender even the most difficult and challenging emotions.

Remaining conscious of our true nature, remembering who we are, these are essential in working with the emotional body. We then can use all of life's experience as a gift to remain in peace and harmony with our intention to live free from personal suffering. Life's manifestations can be used to assist us in living our truth.

EFFORTLESS ENERGY AND THE CHALICE OF LIFE

Effortless energy comes naturally as we move closer to our essential being. We became more at ease and willing to allow our destiny to unfold. Through the Parashakti Breath we release our intense personal striving and return to the simplicity of being.

Our life can be viewed as a chalice of sacred energy that remains full as we release the old and breath in the new. Often, through challenges of life, we deplete our energy, dip into our reserve and become exhausted. We find ourselves no longer rejuvenating because of our inability to breath in our healing light. When we feel our life force being tapped we can learn to use the Parashakti Breath to come into alignment with a greater force that replenishes our system.

The breath is a wonderful tool to learn the action of humility, as we learn that our very breath is a gift from the unseen sacred force in life. The magic of the breath teaches us to be one with the universal flow of the infinite and to float in this holy current of life. Breathing in, we affirm our true nature as infinite beings of freedom. Breathing out, we let go of any holdings of identification that are constricting our freedom. Through the breath we simply let go and relax, allowing the sacred current of our life to take us to our divine home of peace and quiet.

Our chalice remains full and flows over for our use in managing the challenges and lessons of life. When our experiences cause depletion of sacred energy we dip into our reserve, leading to a life of sheer exhaustion. Exhaustion of the vital force comes from our inability to rejuvenate our sacred energy. The chalice is the reserve of our being and must be kept full through awareness and honoring of our true nature. When we find ourselves dipping into our reserve we must take appropriate action to replenish the vital force. All replenishing comes from breathing in and the art of letting go of stress and identification. With breathing as our aid, we can begin the process of revitalization of the life force. Through the awareness of our inner chalice, we must strive to protect it and keep it full at all times.

We must take care of our soul and its divine healing energy as our number one work, allowing our chalice to flow over with love and compassion for the intention of divine service.

VERTICAL BREATHING

Inhale, reach for heaven while firm on the earth. Palms facing forward, stretch your hands above your head as far as possible. Exhale, slowly lower your arms. Relax in a normal standing position. Connect your energies with heaven and earth. This technique straightens the spine and widens the channel for parashakti. Allow the breath to enter through the crown center and flow along the spine, energizing your entire body. Your energy is aligned vertically creating a channel for healing light.

THE PARASHAKTI BREATH

The Parashakti Breath can be used in any place or situation simply by accessing the divine energy found in the sushumna channel. It is a wonderful healing tool, brings peace and light to all areas of the body, mind and emotions. Breathing in, allow your crown center to open to receive this light. Visualize the healing light as coming in through the crown and gently bathing the spinal chakras, moving down the legs and connecting with earth energies.

COLOR BREATHING

Using the suggested breathing techniques bring in color to assist in healing the affected area. Color is a wonderful tool to add to your breathing practice. Common colors used in therapy are:

Red, firey, stimulates the nerves and vitalizes the physical body.

Orange strengthens the vital force and energy of the etheric body.

Yellow the color of the sun, assists the digestive process. It increases the intellect and the power of reason.

Green is the color of healing, cleansing all impurities in the body, mind and emotions. It assists in releasing tension and negative energies. It also regulates the etheric body and stabilizes the astral body.

Blue calms, promotes growth and healing. It is the color of intuition

and connects us to our higher mental body or Buddhic Plane.
Indigo cools, strengthens the thyroid and parathyroid glands. It purifies the blood stream and helps to stop bleeding. It also heals the emotional levels and connects us with the spiritual planes .
Violet purifies the blood, stops the growth of tumors and calms the entire system. When using the violet light or violet flame you can remove negative energy and increase the divine energies in your system.

CIRCLE OF LIGHT BREATHING

Breathe in a white light through the crown center. Exhale and allow this stream of light to move down the front of the body to the feet, cleansing, energizing the chakras, organs, spine and your energy field. Inhale and bring the life force breath through the bottom of the feet, up the back of the body and along the back of the neck to the crown center. While exhaling again, allow the breath to flow down the face and along the front of the body to the feet. Connect this light with earth energies and through your inhalation draw in earth energy and bring it slowly up the front of the body to the head. Exhale and release the breath through the crown center.

Visualize the parashakti (divine energy) flushing out all discordant energies. This circular breathing will reenergize, revitalize and rebirth your entire system. It is a powerful grounding technique when used with visualization working with the sacred or grounding cord.

The Parashakti Breath allows you to experience the space between thoughts, the natural pause between breaths. This space is where you meet your sacred essence.

MUDRAS - SACRED HAND POSITIONS

Mudra means to seal or lock. These sacred hand positions can be used to bring balance to the body, mind and emotions and are to seal in our intention. In yoga philosophy each finger correspond to one of the five elements. Each position shows the relationship of the chakras and elements in our hands.

The thumb represents the fire element corresponding to the solar plexus chakra and the adrenal glands.

The index finger represents the air element and corresponds to the heart chakra and the thymus gland.

The middle finger represents the ether element and corresponds to the throat chakra and the thyroid gland.

The ring finger represents the earth element corresponding to the root chakra and the sexual glands.

The little finger represents the water element corresponding to the navel chakra and the pancreas.

In all mudras the fire element or thumb must be included.

Prana Mudra
Vital force mudra.
Improves energy, circulation, eyesight and general health. Increases vital force. Awakens the root chakra.

Join the tips of your little finger, ring finger and thumb, concentrate on your breathing.

Jnana Mudra
Attaining wisdom.
Aids in concentration, meditation, focusing, memory and brain power. Useful for insomnia. Brings a sense of peace, harmony to all aspects of the body and mind.

Touch the tip of the thumb with the tip of the index finger, using for any time relaxation is needed. Fingers are pointing upward.

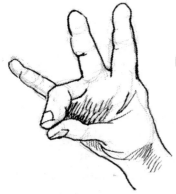

Prithvi Mudra
Increases body energy and flexibility of mind.
Opens the mind, assists one to experience bliss, balances the nutrients of the body. Helps relieve excess energy in the root and navel chakras.

Touch tip of the thumb (fire) to the ring finger (earth) open the rest of the fingers outward.

Apana Mudra
Increases energy.
Useful for all water retention problems, helps to remove toxins from the body. It is a wonderful mudra to assist in the realization of the self.

Join the tip of the thumb (fire) to the tips of the middle and ring fingers (sky and earth).

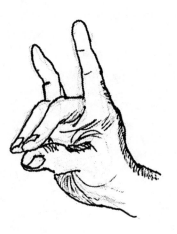

Anjali Mudra
Prayer position.
Namaste or Namaskar, meaning "I salute the divinity within you."

A reverence gesture of respectful greeting. Useful in salutations to another, depicting a great respect, Namaste.

Place your hands together, palms facing. You can use this hand position in front of your heart or in front of your third eye for Namaste salutations and prayer positions.

Dhyana Mudra
For meditation.
Two hands are open and relaxed with the palms
up, resting on the folded legs, the right hand atop
the left with the tips of the
thumbs gently touching.

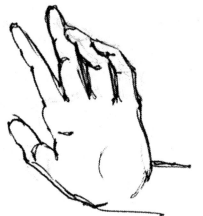

Abhaya Mudra
Seal of divine protection.
Dispels fear and promotes
protection.

Raise your right hand to chest
level with palms facing forward. Place your left hand on your left
thigh, in your lap or on your heart. Use with mantras, visualizations,
prayer, or invocation or with a silent mind.

Shanti Mudra
Invocation of peace seal.
Calms the mind, increases strength and energizes the entire body. Promotes well-being.

Sit in a meditative pose.
Close your eyes and place your hands on your lap, palms facing up and fingers pointing toward each other.
Breathe in, filling your abdomen with air and contracting it. Keep the abdomen contracted and breathe out. Inhale and exhale as deeply as possible.

Concentration: The root chakra (muladhara).
Inhale and fully expand your abdomen. At the same time, raise your hands until they reach your navel again. Coordinate the movement of your hands and abdominal expansion.

Concentration: Breathe from the root center to the navel center. Continue inhaling and expand your chest region by raising your hands to the front of your heart.

Concentration: The solar plexus chakra and the heart chakra. Breathe in and raise your shoulders bringing your hands to the front of your throat.

Concentration: The heart center to the throat center to the third eye center to the crown center.
Retaining your breath, spread your arms to the sides, palms facing up. Holding your breath without any strain, stay in this position for a few seconds.

Concentration: The crown of the head.
As you exhale, lower your arms to the sides and place your hands on your lap. At the end of your exhalation, contract your abdomen and relax your body.

Relax and repeat this mudra exercise, as you desire. Always do deep breathing along with the movement of your arms.

A STUDY OF THE CHAKRAS

Gateways to the Soul
The Senses in Relationship to the Chakras
The Five Elements and the Chakras
The Seven Cosmic Rays and the Chakras

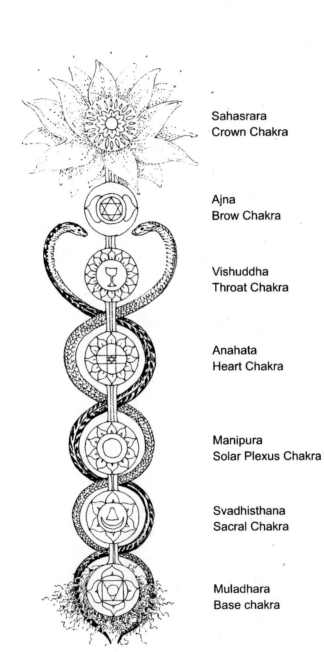

Sahasrara
Crown Chakra

Ajna
Brow Chakra

Vishuddha
Throat Chakra

Anahata
Heart Chakra

Manipura
Solar Plexus Chakra

Svadhisthana
Sacral Chakra

Muladhara
Base chakra

Chapter Ten

GATEWAYS TO THE SOUL
SHIELDS OF LIGHT

The chakras (meaning wheels of light) are whirling centers of vital energy. Each is shaped like a vertical cone. The chakras are found along the spinal cord or sushumna. The sushumna is the energetic channel that runs along the spine from the root chakra located at the base of the spine to the crown chakra, which is at the crown of the head. The chakras function as storage centers, where they energize, control and are responsible for proper functioning of our body, mind and emotions.

Nadis are nerve-like channels that carry our spiritual and vital energies intertwining down the spine like a serpent. The energies flow in a channel from the crown center down the spine to the root center, crossing each other, forming the energy centers or chakras. When the energy paths cross they give the appearance of a lotus with unfolding petals. The number of petals varies according to the number of nadis around the chakras. When the chakra and the petals are facing downward, the energy is undergoing the transformation process. When the petals turn upward they have received the transformational energy needed to proceed in their ascension process.

The path of return is a journey through consciousness. Each chakra plays a vital role in our evolving nature. During our upward journey the energy of our physical being strives to integrate and unite with our spiritual being. The chakras below the heart move in a counterclockwise manner in response to the downward pull of earth's gravity. This downward pull is related to identification with earth energies of survival, power and the false nature of the self. The lower chakras purpose is to turn clockwise in harmony with the upper chakras. This occurs when there are applications of pure will, pure desire and devotion, turning toward our sacred divine nature and aligning all energies with the intention of freedom.

Upon awakening to our true self, the light of our consciousness pierces the center of the chakra involved opening to its divine essence. Each chakra contains a lesson of transformation and has a deep and profound purpose – to assist us on our path.

The gateways to our soul are our centers of light and protection, allowing accumulated energy to exist or enter the system under the direction of soul power. The chakras play an important role in the physical, etheric, or astral, mental and spiritual planes of consciousness. They are our gateway to understanding ourselves on all levels and invite us to integrate our physical nature with our emotional, our emotional with our mental and our mental with our spiritual. The study of the chakras reveals the vital role they play in protecting our body, mind and spirit from outside negative energy. When the chakras are active they do their job well and protect our being on all levels. When they are closed or blocked they are not able to function properly and we become more susceptible to imbalances in our body, mind and emotions.

There are seven major chakras, four in the body and three in the head. The *root center* is the seat of the physical body, the *navel center* is the seat of the vital body, the *solar plexus center* is the seat of the astral body, the *heart center* is the seat of the lower mental body, the *throat center* is the seat of the higher mental body, the *third eye center* is the seat of the intuitive body and the *crown center* is the seat of the spiritual body.

The solar plexus, navel and root are related to our personality nature and function in relationship to our physical survival, needs and wants. They are also considered our power centers because they control the physical senses as well as activate the desires of clinging, craving, possessing, having and rejecting. The heart chakra is considered the bridge of light between the physical (the centers below the heart) and the spiritual (the centers above the heart). The heart, throat, third eye and crown centers are the transcendental chakras of the soul and the higher mind and are related to our higher self. They function to express, expand and deepen us as integrated beings of light.

When the chakras are blended and integrated they are instruments of divine power and glory. In a state of illumination the chakras are like jewels strung upon the necklace of the sushumna, the life force that flows up the spine.

Our chakras represent our state of consciousness and point to where we need to apply the healing attention of love. They are the tools for transformation, a map to our true self. We must carefully look at the patterns of holding and the memories that are held in the lower chakras. We must be willing to be our own healer, by creating affirmations of release, freedom, forgiveness and healing. When we change our consciousness our chakras naturally open and expand upward. Affirming the qualities of our true self leads us to release the bondage of past misidentification and open our energy system to the new and sacred essence of life.

The first three chakras are the testing zones of our spiritual beings, transforming our weaknesses to strengths and transmuting our limited consciousness to divine consciousness. The lower three chakras hold the memory and impressions of thoughts and emotions that have been geared to our false sense of self. The consciousness of these chakras relates to the striving and protection of the personality self. Through our mistaken identity we often lose ourselves in this struggle to maintain our separate sense of self. The solar plexus chakra provides the key to transforming our personal will into divine will, for it is within that center that the battle between the personality and the divine self takes place. When we let go of the struggle to maintain our separate individual self we open the door to our heart center where we meet our true nature.

The root chakra is our foundation. Firmly rooted in ourselves and trusting in life's process we form the first building block that creates stability and strength in ourselves. We must learn to accept the assignment given by the universe and trust in the process of expressions of the root center. Through our relationship with our God center or crown chakra, we infuse our being with trust and security from a long lasting source.

After creating a strong foundation in the root center, we journey into the consciousness of the navel chakra. This is the chakra of our physical vitality and expression in the physical world with our feeling self. It opens and is balanced naturally through the throat chakra.

Using our spiritual chakras assists greatly in healing the chakras of the personality. Working with the ajna chakra, for instance, we create a vision of truth for our being in which we express honor of our true nature. The third eye center is the master center of the personality directing and guiding the energy upward with the purpose of unifying the soul and personality. The surging energy of the navel leads the energy into the stormy seas of the solar plexus chakra. Its partner in transformation is the heart center where our personal will transforms to divine will. The heart center is the energetic bridge of light between the chakras of the personality and the chakras of the soul. Through the healing light of the heart center, we let go and journey from the trappings of personal identification into divine being. When we move from the solar plexus center into the heart center we enter the realm of our Buddha consciousness. This is the center of compassion and love and we no longer walk the path alone. The sacred hand of the divine essence within takes control and we ascend into the spiritual centers of the throat, third eye and crown.

When we transcend the lower chakras and open the doors to our spiritual nature, we become whole and unified. The throat center awakens as we begin to express our truth, divine miracles come from the spoken word. The heart center translates the message of compassion, surrender and letting go through evolving love. The wisdom of the third eye center shines with the light of cosmic consciousness and reveals the universe in its glorified state. The crown center takes its rightful place as the master of all the other centers, integrating and infusing us with divine light.

In this discussion of the chakras we will be focusing on the seven main chakras, which support the physical and etheric energy bodies. There are many more chakras in the energy field such as the alta major chakra that develops through the development of the antahkarana. This is the energetic bridge discussed in previous chapters that is constructed through the union with the personality and the soul. Other important energy centers or chakras are located above the head, the chakra of spirit and below the feet, the chakra of the earth. To keep things simple we will discuss how to remain grounded throughout the ascension process as well as how to stay connected with divine essence by keeping the spirit and grounding chakras balanced.

In addition to the seven chakras we have twenty-one minor centers located throughout our system. Chakras are located in front of each ear, above each breast, where the breast bones meet, in the palm of each hand and the sole of each foot, behind each eye, the gonads in men and the ovaries in women, the liver, the stomach, two near the spleen, behind each knee, the vagus nerve and close to the solar plexus center.

Chapter Eleven

SENSES, ELEMENTS, SEVEN COSMIC RAYS
INTERACTIONS

Our real essence, the divine spark within, communicates through our senses. On each plane we have senses. These gifts from nature for perception of the spiritual world and conscious functioning allow us to act in relationship to our true nature. Our senses look to objects through hearing, touch, sight, smell and taste.

The senses of our human nature stem back to the beginning of creation. Sense development occurred in the following order.

- The sense of hearing was developed in the first root race called the polarian race.
- In the second root race, the hyperborean race, the sense of touch, related to the fourth ether, was developed.
- The third root race, the lemurian race, developed the sense of sight, related to the second ether.
- The fourth root race, known as the atlantean race, developed the sense of taste, which is also related to the second ether.
- The fifth root race, the present aryan race, developed the sense of smell, related to the first ether.

The five physical senses on the physical/etheric plane of hearing, touch, sight, taste and smell are related to our progress in evolution. On each plane of consciousness there are five senses, which are the counterparts or subtler forms of our physical senses.

- The evolution of the astral plane results in development of the astral senses: clairaudience, psychometry, clairvoyance, imagination and emotional idealism.

- The evolution of the mental plane results in the development of the senses of higher clairaudience, planetary psychometry, higher clairvoyance, discrimination and spiritual discernment.
- On the Buddhic plane the higher senses related to the physical are hearing-comprehension, touch-healing, sight-divine vision, intuition-taste and smell-idealism.
- Atmic senses are hearing-beatitude, touch-active service, sight-realization, taste-perfection and smell-all knowledge.

Through the evolution of the senses on each plane we are able to evolve to the next plane. Each plane when fully developed allows a free-flow of energy to the next plane. Consciousness from the emotional interpenetrates the mental, the mental interpenetrates the causal or spiritual and the spiritual interpenetrates the Buddhic and so forth. When building the rainbow bridge (antahkarana), the connecting thread between the lower and higher worlds, each sense is developed on the higher planes as shown above.

We become more attuned to our higher senses through mastery of our lower senses. Through stillness of mind and emotion, higher qualities are developed, resulting in activation of higher faculties or senses.

Senses are gifts of perception, which aid in becoming aware of our surroundings or environment. They demonstrate, according to Alice Bailey, five areas of development:

- The realizations of self-consciousness, personality or *I* consciousness.
- The ability to assert the I consciousness.
- Means to self-conscious evolution.
- A source of knowledge.
- A unifying faculty of the three worlds.

Through understanding the senses we can learn about the evolution of the human being. Within our sense development we strengthen consciousness and therefore ward off incoming disease and disharmony. This power to control the energies that are filtered through the spiritual, mental, emotional and physical-etheric vehicles is the key to mastery. Through our evolvement into our higher nature we learn to master the aspects of our nature that control us. The senses are tools for perception to be used at will. According to the *Bhagavad Gita*, "After acquiring a body, when the indweller wants to leave it, he takes to his senses and goes away, as the wind carries away the fragrance from flowers."

The senses are nature's gift to convey information from the three lower worlds to the higher mental plane. Our true self learns to expand from one plane to another, discriminating between what is real and not real, through sense development. We must gain control of the senses on the physical in order to take the next step in gaining control of the astral plane senses.

An important sense within the Buddhic plane is the sense of intuition, located in the third eye. When this sense is developed, we will have etheric vision at which time we are enlightened or illumined. This is called the eye of the human soul or eye of Shiva.

THE FIVE ELEMENTS AND THE FIVE SENSES

The five elements existed before creation. They appeared in a mysterious succession through the process of evolution. From the radiant sun appeared the original element the akasha or ether, from the ether appeared air and from air, fire originated. The element of water came from fire and from water, the element earth.

In these five great elements the senses were created. Sound is the sense of ether, touch is the sense of air, form is the sense of fire, taste is the sense of water and smell is the sense of earth. Thus sound is the first primordial expression. From there descends touch, then form, then taste and smell. Earth is all the senses combined; smell, taste, form, touch and sound.

THE SEVEN COSMIC RAYS AND THE CHAKRAS

The seven rays are a persons's innate characteristics. Each one of the seven rays is in our makeup but one ray predominates in each of us. This dominant ray is more evolved than others and is considered the individual's ray type.

The seven rays are considered the sum total of the divine consciousness, destined for divine purpose. The number seven is deeply rooted in the physical to which the rays correspond. There are the seven centers in the brain, the seven centers of force (chakras) and the seven major glands, which determine the quality of the physical body. The human in its nature is a sevenfold being with the potential of seven states of consciousness. Each human being has a particular ray quality which has been swept into manifestation by the impulse of one of these rays. These seven rays exist in the cosmos and are essentially white light, but when they hit the human atmosphere they become a prism of many colors. The seven rays may be looked at as channels through which all energy flows. Everything in the solar system that has a living quality to it belongs to one of the seven rays.

The first, second and third rays are the rays of aspect, the fourth, fifth, sixth and seventh rays are the rays of attribute. The first ray is the higher counterpart of the seventh, the second is the higher counterpart of the sixth, the third is the higher counterpart of the fifth and the fourth connects the higher and lower rays and harmonizes them. The rays correspond closely to the chakras.

According to occult sciences color is actually vibratory waves that come from the rays of the great central sun. The seven cosmic rays constitute the seven types of human temperaments.

THE ASPECTS OF THE COSMIC RAYS

First Ray: Monadic plane, crown center, color white or electric blue, gemstone diamond. The qualities of the first ray are power, will, courage, leadership and self-reliance. The aspirations of the first ray are to conquer, to attain and to find ultimate reality. The weaknesses of the first ray are tyranny, self-will, pride, domination, selfishness and thirst for power. The sources of suffering for the first ray are defeat, degradation, humiliation and displacement. The methods of achievement of highest attainment are concentration, will power and discipline

Second Ray: Buddhic plane, heart center, color golden yellow, azure blue, gemstone sapphire. The qualities of the second ray are universal love, wisdom, insight, intuition, sense of oneness, compassion and cooperation. The aspirations of the second ray are to save, to heal, to illumine, to teach, to share and to serve. The weaknesses of the second ray are sentimentality, sensuality, impracticability and unwise self-sacrifice for others undermining their self-reliance and increasing their selfishness. The sources of suffering are heartbreak, loneliness, isolation, exclusion, neglect, broken faith and trust, misjudgment and disloyalty.

Third Ray: Etheric plane, navel center, color emerald green, gemstone emerald. The qualities of the third ray are: creative idealism, comprehension, understanding, mental power, dignity, adaptability and impartiality. The aspirations of the third ray are creative activity and understanding. The weaknesses of the third ray are indecision, seeing too many sides, coldness, cruelty and failure to support in a crisis, deliberate deceit, intrigue and cunning. The sources of suffering are indignity, proven incompetence, darkness.

Fourth Ray: Physical plane, root center, color bronze or red, gemstone jasper. The qualities of the fourth ray are stability, harmony, balance, beauty and rhythm. The aspirations of the fourth ray are to beautify. The weaknesses of the fourth ray are moods of exaltation and despair, sensuousness, posing, self-conceit, self-indulgence. The sources of suffering are frustration and failure to express perfectly.

Fifth Ray: Mental plane, throat center, color yellow, gemstone topaz. The qualities of the fifth ray are analytical, logical, accuracy and patience. The aspirations of the fifth ray are to discover and a thirst for knowledge. The weaknesses of the fifth ray are self-centeredness, smallness of vision, pride, criticism, materialism, separating, one-track mind. The sources of suffering are mental defeat and scorn.

Sixth Ray: Emotional plane, solar plexus, color red, gemstone ruby. The qualities of the sixth ray are one-pointedness, fiery enthusiasm, devotion, loyalty and sacrificial love. The aspirations of the sixth ray are to serve, to adore, to worship the cause. The weaknesses of the sixth ray are: being overemotional, impulsiveness, intolerance, narrowness and blind devotion to personalities, fanaticism and sensuality. The sources of suffering are disloyalty of those who were loved and trusted, being misunderstood and judged, melancholy.

Seventh Ray: Atmic plane, ajna center, color purple, gemstone amethyst. The qualities of the seventh ray are grace, precision, ordered beauty and activity, chivalry, skill, dignity, careful attention to detail and splendor. The aspirations of the seventh ray are to harness, to synthesize, to make manifest. The weaknesses of the seventh ray are formalism, love of power, using people as tools, extravagance, plausibility, regimentation. The sources of suffering are humiliation, loss of power, frustration, rudeness and discourtesy.

INTERACTION OF THE CHAKRAS, PLANES AND RAYS

Chakra	Elem.	Ray	Sense	Quality	Astral	Mental	Intuitional
Root	Earth	1st	Smell	Action	Idealism	Spiritual discernment	Idealism
Navel	Water	2nd	Taste	Reproduction	Imagination	Discrimination	Intuition
Solar plexus	Fire	3rd	Sight	Desire	Clairvoyance	Higher clairvoyance	Divine vision
Heart	Air	4th	Touch	Divine love	Psychometry	Planetary psychometry	Healing
Throat	Sound	5th	Sound	Creativity	Clairaudience	Higher clairaudience	Comprehension
Third eye	Sixth sense	6th		Wisdom	Sixth sense	Intuition	Divine perception
Crown		7th		Divine will	Synthesis	Thought	Pure consciousness

The following chart describes the uses of color healing. The source of this information is S. G. J. Ousely, *The Powers Of The Rays: The Science of Colour Healing,* as described by Zachary Lansdowne,

COLOR HEALING CHART

Color	Description	Illnesses
Red	Heating, vitalization and stimulating vibration.	Blood-deficiency diseases, anemia, physical debility, exhaustion, bad circulation, paralysis and consumption.
Orange	Warm, positive and stimulating color, influencing primarily the vital processes of assimilation and circulation.	Nervous and mental debility, asthma, bronchitis, phlegm and epilepsy.
Yellow	A positive magnetic vibration with a tonic effect on the nerves.	Dyspepsia, diabetes and constipation.
Green	A vibration of harmony and balance...Soothing and sympathetic, it does not excite, inflame or irritate.	Heart complaints, blood pressure and headaches.
Blue	Cold vibration with astringent and sleep inducing properties.	Laryngitis, sore throat, hoarseness, goitre, fevers, palpitation, bilious attacks, colic, jaundice, skin abrasions, cuts and burns.
Indigo	Expels the negative elements in the consciousness.	Deafness, cataract, delerium tremens, eye inflammation, pneumonia,and nervous disorders.
Violet	Corresponds with the highest elements in man's nature.	Nervous ailments, insomnia, mental disorders and cataract.

ROOT CHAKRA MEDITATION

The journey begins deep in the stillness of your being. The first chakra offers a map, holding the memory of
your ancient past and opening your path to uncharted terri-
tories. Through the breath, allow your body to move into a
state of relaxation, inhale opening the crown center and
bring the breath down the spine into the base center, the
home of your foundation. Visualize your spine as a channel for energies to travel, feel your breath flowing up and
down the spine. Now bring your awareness into the root
center where you feel a warm ball of energy, the source of
your life force. From this source you are created and your
birthright is to live, to be happy, secure and trust in life's
processes. Your foundation strengthens as you affirm life's
purpose and fully embrace your unlimited potential.

AFFIRMATION OF GROUNDING
I consciously accept life's assignment to live, evolve and
actualize my soul's gifts. I begin my journey to awaken my full
potential as a divine human being.

Chapter Twelve

THE ROOT CHAKRA
SHIELD OF THE PHYSICAL PLANE

The first chakra or root center, named *muladhara* in Sanskrit (mula meaning root and adhara meaning support); is the foundation for the evolution of our life force. Located at the base of the spine, it opens downward toward the earth with the purpose of receiving earth energies. This center is related to the physical plane, the center of the will to live and the survival instinct. The root center is the support system for all other chakras and is the center for the will to be.

According to the work of Alice Bailey, the serpent of God at the base of the spine goes through two major transformations. The life force ascends up the spine through the sushumna channel to the crown chakra. The serpent of matter lies coiled and is transformed into the serpent of wisdom, which is translated and becomes the "Dragon of Living Light."

As the Kundalini energy awakens in our consciousness with its transformative energy, we begin our ascension from the root center to the crown center. The energy of this chakra is what propels the activation of returning karma, the pathway that leads us to the realization of our true nature. We enter the school of divine consciousness when we let go and trust in life's process. The root chakra is the first classroom where we learn about becoming centered, grounded and solid in relationship to our self. Through returning to the quiet, deep stillness of the root chakra we tap into the strength needed for all experiences in life.

When we have a strong foundation in our root center we become a willing participant in physical existence, cooperating with the forces of mother earth. The root center is where we hold the information about our family of origin, ancestral memories and the memories of our experiences from birth to about eight years old. When our basic needs have not been met in early childhood we often become disconnected from life sometimes attracting a serious physical illness. This disconnection can be healed at any age through affirming our purpose and value as an evolving self.

When our roots are firmly planted in this center we embark on the path of return to our divine being. In consciousness we return to the root of our existence and ground our life force. The lessons of the root center teach us that we need to release old programs and conditioning that retain our energy in an un-transformed state. When we release we can allow life's gifts to be showered upon us in honor or our precious and sacred souls. Beginning with the root chakra we learn to stand on our feet and walk into the world. Reaffirming our sense of trust and safety with our life's processes and lessons builds an inner foundation of strength that is unconditional in relationship to our past experiences. When identified with our insecurities we view ourselves as victims of circumstance. This victim consciousness continues to attract experiences that lead to disempowerment. We become vulnerable in our relationships and experiences in life. Creating a strong foundation for being requires us to reaffirm our sense of self that is not reliant on physical security. In reality, our true, eternal nature is free from all outside experiences and is found through letting go of conditioning that has layered our sense of self.

The root center is our center of vitality where the Kundalini fire assists our energy being to surge upward, transforming the other centers. The home of our basic instincts, this center drives us to find sexual unity, passion and the fire of life. This fire gives a sense of stability, power and base instinct to survive. Through the power of the root center, we manifest our life's experiences, deepening our relationship with joy and gratitude for being alive. A vortex of our primal force, this center can create or destroy. When our energies are positive, optimistic and life affirming, the root center is balanced. When we feel disconnected, scattered and not present in life, we are not in balance. The root chakra strives to be in harmony with the spiritual centers, by reaching for the divine and yet stabilizing and grounding on the earth. Through self-mastery and the development of a strong sense of trust in life's processes, this chakra remains opened.

When this chakra is weak it manifests self-centeredness, anger and fear rooted in the survival instinct. Worry is an expression of an unbalanced root chakra; feeling insecure in the world, everyday life tends to feel burdensome. Emotional confidence, trust, safety, being grounded are deep aspects of this chakra. It is also a reflection of the collective unconscious. The root chakra is expressed in either self-gratification (using life for self-interest or survival) or selfless energy (using this life as an opportunity to serve for the greater good for oneself and all concerned.)

In order to maintain balance, the root chakra should always be in harmony with the third eye and crown chakra. Our spiritual centers offer a sense of purpose for being, understanding and intuiting life's experience. Through working with the higher centers in our transformation process we create a new sense of grounding, a deep connection with the purpose of life. The crown center brings a security that is everlasting as it connects us with the divine creator of life. The third eye center brings our clear vision and connects us with the wisdom to tell the real from the unreal.

Within the root chakra a strong foundation is formed where we develop an inward relationship to life, nature and trust in the process of life. When this energy is purified, it moves in accordance with divine will as it ascends up the spine into the crown chakra. The root chakra holds the lowest vibration of solidness, stability and stillness, creating the fundamental groundwork for our development. When the energy of the root chakra is weak, the physical constitution may reflect it, showing both physical and emotional weakness.

Often in spiritual seeking, higher chakras are developed to the detriment of the lower ones. When we try to jump ahead in our development without the necessary grounding, we lack the stability to open our higher chakras. This can be disturbing and somewhat dangerous on the path of spiritual development. When we begin the deep process of trusting ourselves we will look at life as a school for our highest good and learn the lessons needed to assist our evolution through the chakras.

Through our development we find that we must have a deep grounding in our body, creating a strong and healthy sense of self. This grounding of our being opens the door where we can journey deeper into our consciousness of light and truth. The journey requires an alignment of our personal will with the will of the greater good or the divine. When we are firmly rooted in our energy we are nourished with humility, security, trust and knowingness creating a foundation in which to expand.

THE ROOT CHAKRA CHART

Muladhara - Meaning the keeper of the beginning, the bearer of the foundation, the support at the root

Location - Base of spine between anus and genitals

Physical Correspondence - Bones, skeletal structure, spine

Physical Dysfunctions - Sciatica pain. Lower back pain

Subtle Body - Physical/Etheric

Glandular Connection - Adrenals, controls all solid parts, spinal column, bones, teeth, nails, anus, rectum, colon, prostate, glands, blood, building of cells

Emotional Plane - Primary emotion - fear - released through a deep sense of security and trust; depression, confusion, feeling off centered, not belonging, obsessions released through a deep sense of stillness.

Mental Plane - A strong sense of self, secure with little or no self doubt; stillness

Color - Fiery red

Petals - 4

Element - Earth

Symbol - Elephant of earthly abundance and good fortune, four red petals around a square containing a downward pointing triangle that represents the relationship to earth energies and karma

Animal Correspondence - Elephant

Sense - Smell

Fragrance - Cloves, cedar, patchouli, myrrh, musk

Ayurvedic oils - Ginger, vetiver

Healing Stones - Agate, hematite, blood jasper, garnet, ruby, hematite, bloodstone, smoky quartz, onyx, tiger eye

Sounds - Vowel C spoken in lower c

Mantra - LAM

Words to create healing affirmations - Responsibility, nurturance, abundance, trust, security, safety, stability, oneness, unity, connection with source, empowerment (letting go of being a victim), boundaries, limitations

Verb Word - To have

Yoga Postures - Bridge Pose, Half Locust, Full Locust, Head to knee pose

Balanced chakra: Secure relationship with the earth, loving life, feeling trust and security in oneself, life energy intact, expressing inner strength, achievement of goals and deep trust in life's processes. Inner gratitude; life energy intact.

Unbalanced chakra: Thought and emotions revolve around self interest which focuses on material possessions, security, survival issues, and sensual indulgences such as food, drink and sex; pursuit of desires at any cost, having difficulty in receiving or giving, tendency to maintain distance with others. Distrust of life's processes and feeling ungrounded.

NAVEL CHAKRA MEDITATION

Breathing deeply, allow your awareness to move from the deep stillness of the root center into the navel area, the source from which you express creative physical energy. You have emerged from solidness of the root center, your foundation, into the liquid and flowing energy of the navel, representing change and duality. It is within this center that you connect with the physical world on a feeling level. The navel center offers the energies of play and wonder for celebrating the natural abundance of life. See yourself now as a dancing light of creative energy, expressing your sense of self through joy and communion with others. You are worthy of living and being and easily accept change as a part of your dance.

AFFIRMATION OF CREATIVE EXPRESSION
I invite my soul to dance in the rhythm of life,
opening, receiving, changing and evolving, with a
spirit of unconditional acceptance.

Chapter Thirteen

THE NAVEL CHAKRA
SHIELD OF THE ETHERIC PLANE

The second chakra, the navel center, is called *svadhisthana* in Sanskrit, meaning dwelling place of the self or sweetness. This chakra is where our emotionally centered self is expressed and is the home of our vital force. The navel center is located at the fifth lower lumbar vertebra area and has to do with vitality, sexual expression and reproduction. The navel center produces and assimilates internal energy received through air and food and distributed from the spleen to the meridians. The task of the navel chakra is to transfer and distribute the vital force throughout all areas of the physical body.

Corresponding to the water element, the second chakra cleanses the body and mind of lower impulses and physical toxins. On the physical level the kidneys and bladder are strengthened and on an emotional level emotions are centered and purified. The water element of the root center frees us from attachment and bondage to our changing nature and the changing nature of our relationships.

When the navel center is in balance it creates a sense of abundance and appreciation for what life brings. The navel center is where the life force produces the energy to ascend on the journey through consciousness. This chakra is considered the seat of Shakti, where our physical, sexual and creative energy is expressed. The navel center is a place of life, of conception, change and movement. It can be visualized as a bright sphere of radiant orange light bringing forth creative energies and ideas.

This center holds the magical wonder of our being and is related to the ages of eight to fourteen, when we most experience life's sweetness and unconditional joy. It can be greatly damaged and blocked due to misuse and misunderstanding of sexual energy resulting in a weakened physical stamina that attracts illness. The transformation of sexual energies occurs when they are channeled through the higher creative expressions of the throat chakra in artistic ways such as dance, music, art and poetry.

In our human nature we long for unity with a part of us that feels separate and split from our source. As we have journeyed from the stillness of the root center into the movement, separation, activity and duality of the navel center, the movement of the navel chakra allows our feeling nature to be expressed outwardly as well as prompting us to return again to be nourished by our life force. Reality is that search to find wholeness and unity is the search for the divine source of our being.

It is within the lower centers that we get caught in the web of illusion and in which we are tested to discern our shadow self from our real self. We discover our true nature by striving to move past our limitations and into the sacred essence of our heart. Through awakening we can ascend past the trappings of the centers of desire and misidentification to open the doors to our eternal nature.

The navel center generates the play of opposites such as the urge to create or to destroy, fear versus truth, the manifestation of healthy or unhealthy life-styles. The changes of life play out in experiences of ups and downs, often moving from pleasurable situations to unpleasant ones. The challenge in this center is the balancing of these opposing forces.

The root center represents change, duality, movement, flexibility and flow. When we energetically tune into this center we can observe that our lives are best served when we flow and experience life in an unconditional manner. This center, when balanced, represents a reservoir of movement, our being is liquid and flowing from moment to moment and experiences the miracle of life. The miracle is that we are on a sacred path of return to our divine source. Surrender of our limitations leads us to this possibility.

We are on a journey of ascension, the path of return to our true nature, moving through our limitations into greater and greater aspects of our true nature. Each chakra represents a crossroad in our transformation in which the path opens to the next school of consciousness. We have the opportunity to investigate what our intentions are in this life, often pointing to transforming desires that are geared toward self-gain and desires that serve our intention of truth and freedom.

The navel center is depicted as a six-petal lotus that relates to the six passions of lust, anger, greed, deceit, pride and envy. Through mastery we have the potential of overcoming these qualities and open to our full potential as human beings. The transformation of these emotions assists us in the evolution to our heart center.

When working with the second chakra we learn to transcend and transform our desires and passions in order to move to the next level of consciousness. The lessons of these desires and passions lie deep within our subconscious mind, which is programmed to seek a familiar pleasurable experience stored in our memory.

The ajna center is the master center of the body and works closely with the energies of the navel chakra. Awakening our inner eye we develop discernment, which assists us in mastering the challenges found in the navel center. Our inner eye creates a direct stream of consciousness within the navel center where emotions, desires, pleasures and feelings are integrated with our higher knowing and our intention for wholeness. We begin our awakening through listening to the sound of our inner voice.

THE NAVEL CHAKRA CHART

Svadhisthana - Meaning sweetness; self-abode where the vital force resides

Location - Lower lumbar area, lower abdomen, between navel and genitals

Physical Correspondence - Sex organs, bladder, kidney, circulation system, vital force, sacral plexus, sacral vertebra, liquids of the body

Physical Dysfunctions - Kidney, bladder problems, circulation and skin issues, lower back pain, sex organs, small intestine.

Subtle Body - Etheric

Glandular Connection - Ovaries, testicles, reproductive organs; controls pelvic area, sex organs, potency, fluid functions, kidneys and bladder

Emotional Plane - Desire, passion; ability to be comfortable with feelings, good self-esteem, healthy sexual attitude, physical creativity. Emotional instability

Mental Plane - Emotional principle, manas, which work through the senses; understanding the duality of the world, working with opposites

Color - Orange

Petals - 6

Element - Water

Symbol - White crescent moon- six orange petals containing a second lotus flower and a crescent moon

Animal Correspondence - Makara - a fish tailed alligator, fish and sea creatures

Sense - Hearing

Fragrance - Ylang, ylang, sandalwood, jasmine and rose

Ayurvedic Smell - Cedar, sage, patchouli

Healing Stones - Carnelian, moonstone, citrine, topaz, coral, tourmaline

Sounds - Sound and Vowels O sung in D

Mantra - VAM

Words to create healing affirmations - Happiness, fulfilled, acceptance of self and others, worthy, creative, expressive, honor, nurture, listen to feelings, working in harmony with truth and inner vision, vital energy intact, moving freely with ease through the world, acceptance of change

Verb Words - I feel, I open, I am

Yoga Posture - Pelvic Rock, Leg Lifts, Hip Circles

Balanced Center - Harmonious feelings, healthy sexual feelings, flowing with the creative energy of life; expressing physically, emotionally and mentally; physical action is creative. Second chakra opens when we have the ability to feel pleasure and pain, letting go of past fears, disillusion and disappointed memories. We use our energy to unite with another, giving emotional support without condition. Happily connected with life, good self- esteem.

Unbalanced Center - Unhealthy relationship with our sexuality stemming from puberty, judgment regarding our sensuality, loss of innocence and wonder regarding the magic of life. Conscious mind is uncomfortable with painful or powerful feelings. We seek union at any cost, using lovers to fulfill our deep longing to unite with the other half of our soul.

SOLAR PLEXUS CHAKRA MEDITATION

Allow your awareness to move into your solar plexus center. Breathing deeply, exhale, letting go of all concerns and worry. With inhalation, reaffirm the peace and lightness of your true nature. Your journey into manifestation leads from the formation of self into the expression of self through power and opinions. Observe your sense of self here, along with thoughts and emotions arising and disappearing. Gently bring your breath into these passing states and relax into the peace of your true nature. Breathing deeply, allow your consciousness to expand beyond the limitation of your thoughts and emotions. In the solar plexus center, transform your desires into divine aspirations. It is here you are empowered through taking responsibility for your divine self.

AFFIRMATION OF POWER
I transform all energies from the lower frequencies
of my self-limitation, into the higher frequencies
of my divine potential.

Chapter Fourteen

THE SOLAR PLEXUS CHAKRA
SHIELD OF THE EMOTIONAL PLANE

The third center, or solar plexus chakra, is called *manipura* meaning lustrous gem in Sanskrit. This fire center receives and distributes energy throughout the physical form. Located in the abdominal region with the sacral and base centers below the diaphragm and the throat and heart centers above the diaphragm, this center can be thought of as the clearing house for the two centers below. It is considered the organ of desire, where we are challenged to transform our self-centered desires into divine aspirations.

The solar plexus center is related to the ages between fourteen and twenty-one years. This is the time in life where the desire self seeks to become integrated with the higher visions of the soul, often creating a sense of inner turbulence. This chakra is also called the sea of turmoil, because of the stormy seas we have to endure on the path of return (emotional life, desires and instinctual feelings). The average person, and our society as a whole, is working through the solar plexus chakra at this time. Most people are deeply conditioned to fulfill desires, seek personal power and build a false sense of self. Through contact with the heart center we learn to soften the hardness of our personal drives and taste the gentleness of our spirit.

By turning our desires into aspirations we journey into our spiritual centers and activate their divine teachings. The third eye center is particularly helpful in assisting us to see the end result of seeking self-gratification, pointing us to see what is real and what is unreal. An affirmation that assists in calming this center is "I have all I need and more, my power comes from the source."

The solar plexus chakra is the organ of synthesis and the mechanism of control and decision-making. This center represents a quest for personal power as all energies that are related to desire and will for earthly life accumulate here. When this center becomes confused with power issues, the struggle to become an individual takes on self-centered qualities. Our true empowerment comes from developing a sense of responsibility for our spirit natures, while listening to our intuition.

As energy travels into the heart center we become purified, cleansed and energized with the love and service aspects of our spiritual heart. Through the heart center we have the opportunity to align our self with our divine consciousness and unite with the higher intention of our soul. Within our sacred heart we learn life's divine principles of discernment, love, compassion, forgiveness, surrender, understanding and so on. Through the transformation of the energies of the solar plexus center into the heart, the petals reach upward building a bridge of light pulling the energies up from the lower centers and uniting them with the higher centers.

After crossing the bridge of light, the emotions in the solar plexus center that are directed toward self-centeredness become emotions of harmlessness, service and love. These higher emotions are revealed when we turn our attention inward to our sacred heart, the dwelling place of our true self. When we journey into our heart chakra we begin to experience a new found peace and calmness in our lives

The battle of our life often is most felt in the solar plexus where the lower self struggles to maintain its position and power at all cost. In the region of the solar plexus we experience tightness and exhaustion due to these personal struggles. This occurs when there is a strong identification with the wants and needs projected by the personal self, resulting in an overwhelming tiredness. When the effort created through trying to maintain control, power and position in life becomes too great, we must let go and let God, bringing an end to our personal struggles.

The deep calling of our true nature awakens in our heart center as well as a yearning to unite with our divine source. The path of return leads us through the gateway of the solar plexus beyond the grip of our self-centered identity. We meet our inner guide in the sanctuary of the heart where all our feelings and emotions are integrated into our being. In the sanctuary of the heart we find the eternal security to let go of the past, as well as the layers of identification with the false nature of the self.

When we are under the influence of our personal will and identify with the personality, this chakra reflects a yellow color that represents the thought process. When transcending the personal self and allowing the wisdom of our true nature to come forth, this chakra reflects a golden color of wisdom and abundance.

The solar plexus is our guide to the world around us and can provide an important protective force until our inner light becomes completely balanced. This chakra represents the great fire of purification burning the desires and wishes of our lower nature. It can allow the spiritual riches of our true self to manifest in the material world. This chakra, when balanced and opened, brings us inner joy, surrender and lightness. When this chakra is disturbed we feel depressed, a sense of hopelessness; we are affected by the illness of separation, striving and personal power.

The solar plexus chakra is the chakra of photography; discriminating, repelling, magnifying, reflecting the duality of thoughts and emotions. It is a connecting link to the mental and spiritual planes of consciousness. The solar plexus receives information from the mental and higher mental and translates it through the chakras of the heart and throat. It also receives information from the physical and etheric planes and translates them through the root and navel chakras. It is the feeling center of the body and it picks up on the energy of others; for this reason it can be thought of as a transmitting tool, accessing information from the lower and higher planes.

In the solar plexus center we strive to cultivate a sense of inner security. We look for ways of feeling powerful in the outer world, often manipulating life to achieve our desires. When we reach the end of this cycle of cause and effect we begin to turn our attention away from the habits of personal striving and seek to understand ourselves in a different way. Our aspirations lead us to find security that is everlasting through the meeting of our eternal and divine nature. This light within becomes our guide as we move from the limitations of the lower three chakras into the heart. It then becomes possible to create a life of happiness, well-being and peace.

THE SOLAR PLEXUS CHART

Manipura - Meaning lustrous gem, city of gems

Location - The well between the shoulder blades (backside) in between the navel and sternum (front side)

Subtle Body - Astral and emotional

Physical Correspondence - Digestive system (particularly liver and small intestine), muscles, stomach, gall bladder, nervous system, pancreas, lower back, physical solar plexus, endocrine glands

Physical Dysfunctions - Allergies, digestive problems, assimilation of energy, nervous system disorders, fatigue, pain in middle and lower back

Glandular Connection - Pancreas and adrenals-controls liver, digestive system, stomach, spleen, gall bladder, autonomic nervous system, lower back, muscles

Emotional Plane - Main emotion: Fear - false sense of power through wrong identification, low sense of self, need to be in control, manipulation, insecurity

Mental Plane - Letting go of unwanted thoughts and accumulation from the past, believing in your true nature, diving into the unknown essence of being, surrendering to the master in the heart. Relates to reasoning faculty.

Color - Golden or yellow

Petals - 10

Element - Fire

Symbol - A ten petaled lotus flower containing a downward-pointing triangle surrounded by three T-shaped swastikas, or Hindu symbol of fire.

Sense - Sight, shaping of being

Fragrance - Peppermint, lemon, rosemary, lavender, carnation, cinnamon, marigold, chamomile, thyme

Ayurvedic Oils - Sandalwood, lavender and fennel

Healing Stones - Citrine, turquoise, lapis, amber, tiger eye, topaz, aventurine, quartz

Sounds - Vowel C spoken in lower c

Mantra - RAM

Words to create healing affirmations - Power, source, divine will, becoming, honor, respect, discernment, receive, surrender, let go, peace, wholeness, purpose, meaning, self will, courage, inner strength

Verbs - I can, I am,

Yoga Postures - Bow Pose, Belly Push, The Woodchopper, Sun Salutation

Balanced Center: Feeling peace and harmony with inner self, actions are performed with a deep reverence for life; light and energy are your expressions. Living for the highest good for all concerned, wishes are fulfilled spontaneously because of the emission of light that you give. You live in a state of protection from negative vibrations with acceptance of others and yourself. Transforming personal power to divine power or will you have the ability to make clear decisions. You have self respect and trust in your intelligence.

Unbalanced Center: There is a mistaken identification of the false nature of the self driven by personal power. Power is used to manipulate life according to self-centeredness. There is a lack of genuine self-worth. Disturbance comes often because of emotions held from deep within. Striving, positioning and aggression are expressions of a sense of low self-worth; as are fear of failure, unworthiness and using power for self-gain.

HEART CHAKRA MEDITATION

Enter the heart center through forgiveness and love, releasing your ties to the past. The doorway through the heart asks you to leave the burdens of your worldly mind behind. Breathing deeply, sink into your true reality of peace. Within the heart center, visualize a beautiful altar where you surrender all pain of separation and personal striving. Allow the breath to assist you to release all discordant energies of the personal self, breathing in compassion, forgiveness and healing. Through grace, the veils to your true nature are removed and you celebrate the recognition of your childlike being. Open your heart center deeper and deeper to your divine reality; see yourself as the essence of the whole, no longer a fragment of self.

AFFIRMATION OF LOVE

Love is my true essence, the fuel for my journey,
I allow love to heal, forgive, bring compassion to all
aspects of my being and I extend this sacred
love to all who cross my path.

Chapter Fifteen

THE HEART CHAKRA
SHIELD OF THE MENTAL PLANE

The Heart is the only reality, the mind is a transient phase, and to remain as one's self is to enter the heart.

Sri Ramana Maharshi

The fourth or heart chakra is called *anahata* meaning pure in Sanskrit and is located between the shoulder blades at the level of the heart. It is the source of all light and love; and is related to the ages of twenty-one to twenty-eight years. The heart is the center of transformation where the lower chakras and the higher chakras meet and become integrated, creating oneness of being. The heart center opening demonstrates the deepest action of love turned inward. This action transcends the ego and is the first step in dissolving the separate sense of self created by the mind. Through tuning the mind with our heart, we become aligned with our soul light; this light flows into the heart center creating energy of radiant love.

The heart represents the meeting ground for the spiritual triad of love, will and wisdom. This meeting occurs when the head center becomes the point of contact for spiritual will, the heart center becomes the agent for spiritual love and the throat center becomes the expression of the spiritual mind. The personality becomes soul-infused with divine essence, allowing our highest nature to come through.

The opening of the heart center occurs through the awakening of our authentic self, letting go of the personality tendencies of the lower three chakras that often are expressed as anger, depression, arrogance, desperation and emotional insecurity. The emotional deviations held within the heart from past traumatic memories tend to deplete the heart of its vital force. Many die of a broken heart, unable to mend the pain of emotional trauma. Because this chakra is closely associated with the thymus gland, which governs the immune system, it is quite vulnerable to our emotional health. This chakra functions to protect, heal and bring balance to the body, mind and emotions. To be well emotionally we must call our spirit back to this moment and free ourselves from the holdings of the past. Through infusing our being with the qualities of love, forgiveness and compassion it is possible to free the frozen energies that are trapped by the past.

The heart center is a bridge of light between the lower centers and the higher ones that we must all cross when moving from the limited consciousness of the personality to our divine consciousness. The bridge of light requires letting go of the past and opening our hearts to the sacred essence of the divine.

The heart functions to forgive and let go of memories that bind us to the past. The forgiveness process opens the door to true compassion for our life and our relationships. In this process we take responsibility for our selves and our actions in relationship to our false identification. The motto "Do unto others as you would have them do unto you," is the essence of balanced heart chakra. We also see that those who have trespassed against us did so out of ignorance. "Father forgive them for they know not what they do," is the essential teaching of Christ, showing that we must learn to forgive ignorance. We see that our trespasses must also be forgiven for they were done out of the same ignorance.

The forgiveness process creates the miracle of transformation where we understand that love is forgiving and we truly let go of blaming others for our life's situation. We strive to become the cause of our life, seeing the seeds of desire and want before they manifest. The play of cause and effect in our life is lessened as we turn within and look at the source of desire, seeking and wanting. The key to true happiness is to live with an unconditional relationship to life, ending all seeking, wanting and grasping.

The heart center opens when the personal will is transformed to divine will and our personal power evolves to an empowered heart. Our heart becomes devoted to being in peace, giving and receiving love and practicing the art of discernment. We learn to live in unconditional love and compassion towards others and ourselves. We also learn to give from our overflow, cherishing and hold our sacred energy. Through a balanced heart chakra we experience the living qualities of beauty, wisdom, forgiveness and acceptance of self and others as we are.

The gateway into our heart of light opens through transforming our personality to the level of our true nature. We have the great task of seeing through the illusion of the astral plane. This is the portal where our un-awakened ego self clings to the material world, feeding off the drives, urges, glamours and illusions and tendencies for future births.

The heart center opens through surrender of our separate sense of self. The doorway leads us to meet our inner lord, our beloved guide. This is the beloved sage within who has walked beside us through all our life's experiences. The ignorance of our lower self (personality) has obstructed our meeting with this inner teacher. A great joy is experienced when this conscious meeting takes place. It is most essential to remain in the essence of this divine force through the rest of our journey, holding it sacred. Through our contact with our inner teacher we live our life in spiritual love, wisdom and will, in the rhythm of nature and according to divine law.

In our sacred heart center we drink from the chalice of our inner truth; realizing that our true nature is witness consciousness, observing all that has been, is and will be. We see that we are in the center of this consciousness observing moment to moment the play of time. This consciousness sees the truth and lives without judgment. The heart chakra brings the law of detachment into place, where we let go of our sense of self-importance. The belief in a separate sense of self dissolves in our heart center under the influ-

ence of unconditional love. As we move into deeper and deeper realization of our ever present self we serve the greater good of our
life.

The heart chakra is a chalice of love. As this center deepens
its awakening, it attains the great power of parashakti (divine force)
for transformation and healing of any limitations.

THE HEART INITIATION

When the heart initiation takes place we enter into our Buddhic
light, the vehicle of our soul. The principles of higher consciousness are now the foundation for our being, as our personal will is
now surrendered to the will of God. Through this initiation, Kundalini
energy is unleashed to move freely from its resting place at the base
of the spine upward to the sahasrara chakra at the crown of the
head. This movement of our life force is the marriage of matter and
spirit. The Shakti force at the base of the spine meets the Shiva
force at in the crown center flowing together into the heart center.
Through this union we become soul infused beings; creating a deep
sense of wholeness.

Through the heart initiation we attain the essence of balance
and equanimity within and are no longer affected by the duality of
life. The great downpour of sacred energy occurs from the upper
chakras flooding the lower chakras with divine energy. The heart
initiate is tested in every degree to free the heart from past inclinations toward lust, hate, greed, pride and envy, so that there may be
freedom from selfishness. Through the opening up of the heart center we become spiritual warriors, protecting our sacred energy from
the pitfalls of illusion. Harmlessness is cultivated. The symbol for
the heart chakra is the deer, achieving *ahimsa*, the path of peace in
daily life. As does this gentle deer, the aspirant places his complete
trust in God.

The heart center opening can be painful. It is the cross that we
must bear when leaving our identification with the temporary nature
of life. Through the cleansing of our emotional and the release of
the past the heart center opens.

Center of the Heart
" *Anahata* "

HEART OF LIGHT

THRONE OF WITNESS CONSCIOUSNESS

SEAT OF THE SOUL

TEMPLE OF THE SPIRIT

SOURCE OF DIVINE WISDOM

Services of the Heart

To give rebirth and resurrection in life

To raise vibrations of vehicles to become instruments of the soul

To act as a bridge of light between form and formlessness, becoming a whole human being

To express divine love, peace, joy, service, courage, understanding

The luminous gateway of our heart center leads to the antahkarana or bridge of light, which makes the ascension back to our true home possible. This sacred bridge is energetically constructed through a complete letting go of spiritual ignorance and identification with a separate sense of self.

The heart chakra center is the master station for the polarities of the emotional, mental and etheric bodies. The lower impulses of the chakras of the personality are mastered and transformed to reflect our true essence of divinity. Through initiation into the heart chakra qualities like reverence, service, compassion and selfless love are developed.

Our birth is for the purpose of deepening an awareness of light, expressing the love and wisdom of our true nature. This awareness leads us on a journey in consciousness from the lower chakras, (the organs of the personality) to the higher chakras of the spiritual triad of love, wisdom and spiritual will. The gateway to the heart initiation is opened giving us the protection, devotion and strength to evolve into our eternal consciousness. Letting go of the past with all its memories and sorrows we develop a deep trust and surrender and our heart opens to unconditional love and forgiveness. From this surrender we live in each eternal moment where life is pure and free from all effect of the past.

Our journey takes us into our luminous body of light where we begin a life of service and devotion to the divine. Our true happiness is found through knowing the essence of life, the current of love behind all manifestation. This love is our innermost core, our divine essence.

The song of the heart brings great love, beauty and unbounded joy; it is our divine call on the path of return. This most sacred song is heard in the silence of the heart, teaching us about deep compassion and forgiveness, the healing miracles.

THE FLOWERING LOTUS OF THE HEART

The lotus of the heart is connected to the world through compassion; remaining untouched by all worldly experiences. This most sacred lotus is always flowering in the rhythm of our inner life, releasing the divine nectar of pure love in support of our true nature.

Within the depth of our divine heart is a sacred resting place where we can retreat in silence, knowing this is the reservoir of the love, pure wisdom and guidance of divinity. As each petal unfolds within the heart, the chalice of life is filled with sacred essence. As we journey deeper into the silence of the heart there are greater and greater levels of awareness of our true nature.

The lotus of the heart unfolds deeply as we turn our attention inward, realizing our true nature is pure witness consciousness. Our true nature is always present watching, observing and waiting silently in the seat of our heart.

Through the process of letting go of the false self held in separation and personal power, our heart opens to its natural flowering. Each of the twelve petals of consciousness opens as we become aligned with our soul.

The first petal unfolds when we meet our innermost self within the sanctuary of our heart and awareness turns from identification with the body to knowing our true self.

The second petal opens through realization that we are not our emotions nor our mind. Our true nature is an expression of divinity, found in the heart of goodness, in alignment with inner truth.

The third petal unfolds in the lotus of the heart when our thinking is used for higher aspiration and the mind becomes silent. The mind, having dissolved into the sacred heart, becomes a silent observer and our thoughts transform to intuition, perception and discernment.

The fourth petal opens when we release attachment to the things of this world. The knowledge obtained within our heart's unfolding lotus deepens our understanding of pure consciousness.

The fifth petal unfolds when we are firmly embedded in our true nature, demonstrating steadfastness, vigilance and uncompromising clarity.

The sixth petal unfolds when all that is not of our pure consciousness is burned in the sacred fire of our inner light.

The seventh petal opens when our inner being is adorned with all inclusive love, harmlessness and devotion to the ever-present sacred self that resides in the spiritual heart.

The eighth petal opens when there is a direct perception of our true reality. All doubt is removed from seeing the light of consciousness.

The ninth petal opens when there is deep and profound peace, the past is dissolved completely and true freedom has been realized.

The tenth petal opens when we live fully in each sacred moment, awaiting life's calling to service.

The eleventh petal opens when we experience the joy of our being and share it with others.

The twelfth petal opens when we walk the path of compassion.

THE HEART CHAKRA CHART

Anahata - Meaning un-struck, pure, unbroken; the love chakra

Location - Heart, center of the chest

Physical Correspondence - Thymus, blood, life force, vagus nerve, circulation

Physical Dysfunctions - Heart disease, cancer, high blood pressure, breathing and circulation problems, immune system diseases, skin disorders.

Subtle Body - Mental and higher mental

Glandular Connection - Thymus- controls heart, blood, circulation, immune system, lower lungs, rib cage, skin, upper back, and hands

Emotional Plane - Main emotion: Love - co-dependency, melancholia, loneliness, betrayal, devotion

Mental Plane - Love that is blocked by thought patterns and conditioning. Thoughts that are geared to conditional love based on ideas, things, bargains, comparison, the past, etc.

Colors - Green-healing, pink-divine love

Petals - 12 inside of which are two overlapping triangles forming a six-pointed star, representing the ability of the individual to evolve upward or downward.

Element - Air

Symbol - Lotus of twelve petals, containing two intersecting circles that make up a six pointed star descending toward matter and pointing upward, raising matter toward spirit. Small chakra below heart called Ananakanda Lotus is the celestial wishing tree that holds the deepest wishes of the heart.

Sense - Touch

Fragrance - Attar of roses, bergamot, clary sage, geranium, rose

Ayurvedic Oils - Rose, lavender, sandalwood

Healing Stones - Rose quartz, tourmaline, kunzite, emerald, jade, watermelon tourmaline, azurite, aventurine quartz, malachite, moonstone.

Sounds - Ay as in ray

Mantras - Yam

Associated Animal - Deer, gazelle, antelope

Words to create healing affirmations - Love, compassion, open, receive, accept, forgive, release, surrender, enjoy, joy, peace, harmlessness, unconditional, freedom, sacred, essence, being, honor, worthy, give,

Actions - I love, I accept, I forgive, I release, I am,

Yoga Postures - Cobra, Fish, Windmill, Cow Head pose, Salutation to the Sun.

Balanced Center: When this center is balanced, all centers are in harmony creating a clear channel for Shakti energy. We become an open vessel for the divine and our personal will is deeply surrendered to divine will. When the heart center is open we radiate love, sincerity, happiness and warmth. Compassion becomes the foundation of our true nature, as we no longer feel the separation inherent in the world. We feel alive and joyful in the moment.

Unbalanced Center: Love given from an unbalanced heart center has a conditional quality, expects something in return or recognition of some kind. It is difficult to accept love and support from others; we are not open to receive. Being sensitive and gentle are qualities that feel embarrassing and we build up a defensive mechanism. We can love too much and be co-dependent of love and care for others' needs before our own. When we give love from a disturbed heart center we always worry about rejection and have a tendency toward sadness and depression. The question regarding caring from the heart will always be "What is in this for me?" When our heart center is shut down it will express itself as cold heartedness or heartlessness.

THROAT CHAKRA MEDITATION

As you emerge from the deep cavern of your heart, the wounds of the past are healed through forgiveness and compassion. Your journey of transformation leads you to the school of truth, where you are called to act according to divine reality. You have learned the art of observation and have mastered your wandering self. You see clearly the path of truth and hold steadfast to your vision of return. You are the co-creator of your divine reality. Your journey now asks you to release all residue of judgment, self-doubt and fear. Your divine will is a charioteer leading you to express and manifest the gifts of spirit through beauty, song, dance and celebration.

AFFIRMATION OF TRUTH
I demonstrate the divine spirit in my life
in all my expressions

Chapter Sixteen

THE THROAT CHAKRA
SHIELD OF THE BUDDHIC PLANE

Until one is committed there is hesitancy, the chance to draw back, always ineffectiveness. Concerning all acts of initiative (and creation), there is one elementary truth, the ignorance that kills countless ideas and splendid plans; that the moment one definitely commits oneself, then providence moves too. All sorts of things occur to help one that would have never otherwise occurred. A whole stream of events issues from the decisions, raising in one's favor all manner of unforeseen incidents and meetings and material assistance, which no man could have dreamt would have come his way.

William Hutchison Murray

The fifth chakra or throat center is called *visuddha* in Sanskrit, meaning pure. This center is considered the chakra of miracles. Through our inner truth we become a co-creator of our reality. The throat center reveals the power to create and envision that which works for our highest good and the highest good for all concerned. Related to the ages twenty-eight through thirty-five, this center expresses the creative energy of our spirit.

Our journey in consciousness takes us on the path of return through the limitations of the lower chakras into the higher centers of our true self. When we enter the realm of the throat center we have the opportunity to express the joy of pure being-ness.

The throat center is where we express, receive and transmit information through the voice. It is the power of the throat center that teaches us to use sound, prayer and affirmations for healing and balancing any discord of our body, mind and emotions. A beautiful blue light emanates from this center in various shades according to the vibration of our expression. We connect with our spiritual nature through the ethereal realm of the throat chakra corresponding to the higher mental body. This is the intuitive plane, where we intuit, perceive and manifest our inner being according to our truth.

The fifth chakra is the center of our higher will where we express the essence of wisdom and will from the higher centers and love from the heart center. The gospel of St. John states "In the beginning was the word and the word was with God." This statement refers to the power of manifestation through sound.

The throat chakra is often damaged in early childhood when we are told that children are to be seen and not heard. Years of conditioning not to speak our truth can impact our life in a deep way. We learn through this conditioning to live in fear and self-judgment of our feelings, creating a disconnection between our intellect and heart. The throat center represents the transformational energies where we let go of our fear through contact with our higher centers of love and wisdom. The journey to our spiritual nature purges the unnecessary conditioning in our life. This leads us to turn within our hearts as the true essence of our being, which is untouched by fear.

In a balanced throat center we express ourselves responsibly and harmlessly, and develop the art of inner listening. Through listening to life's messages and expressing our truth we gain the power to transform our life. When we speak with confidence and clarity we create the essence of truth in our lives; when we speak with self-doubt we communicate the message of doubt and insecurity.

The lessons of the throat center teach us about the importance of honesty in all aspects of our life. This requires us to practice discernment at all times, observing the voice of doubt, judgment, self-criticism and other untruths that are held deep within our conditioning. We learn to let go of false accumulations and live in each moment no longer bound by the conditioning of the past.

The throat center is the bridge between the body and the mind, the connection between the feeling nature of our being and the higher wisdom of our sacred spirit. The *antahkarana* or bridge of light is constructed through the transformation of the personality self to the divine self. This occurs when our higher energies move downward through the unified head center and our lower energies move upward through the dual nature of the body creating a unity of being and opening the Sushumna channel of light. As we open the throat center, the clear expression of divine energies and the clear seeing of divine energies create the link between the lower chakras and the crown center.

As we ascend into the true essence of this center, there is a new consciousness of willingness. Letting go of all habits, instincts and patterns of the ego that were based on preservation of the personality self, we now move into the expression of our divine consciousness. We practice the art of surrendering using the motto "Let go and let God" in our daily lives. This leads us to become messengers of spirit; ever-present and willing to be servants of its luminous light.

The highest expression of the visuddha chakra is prayer – the deep communion between the true self and the higher omnipresent force of life. Prayer in this way is the process of ever-deepening devotion and surrender to the highest will of the divine. The throat center is where we take the path of surrender, turning our thoughts and attention inward to the silence of our true self.

When the centers below the throat are balanced, we journey into the chakra of miracles and life is fully lived in the moment. We attain a new found, divine power, the ability to speak the truth, affirm what is necessary for our life and for it to manifest clearly. The saying "Be careful about what you wish for" is very accurate in relationship to the throat center, for it has the power to manifest and create realities based on the spoken word. The highest expression of our true nature is the gift of manifestation, where our deepest wishes are expressed and affirmed and all self-doubt is removed.

The throat chakra is the primary tool in healing, for it is in this center our higher self or Buddhic nature dwells. In relationship to the health of an individual, it is connected to thyroid and parathyroid glands. These glands guard health and metabolize the energy of the system. When we express the truth, believing it to be so, we create an opening for the grace of healing to take place.

THE PATH OF SILENCE

Silence is the unseen power of the throat center, the space in which the creative word is expressed. Silence is the source of healing all imbalances of the body, mind and spirit, realigning us with our inner truth. Silence is the avenue we must take in order to free ourselves from unwanted thought and disturbance that comes from identification with the changing nature of life. It is a great centering device bringing coordination, order and calmness to our daily life. Through silence we build our vital force and keep it as a reservoir for our creative expression. When our life energy is intact, we are able to tap into our creative resources and co-create through our divine guidance.

Silence leads us to our natural state of witness consciousness, the perception of our true reality that is always seeing, observing and being. This seeing leads to perception of how we bring expression into alignment with inner truth. Silence stills our mind, emotions and bodily sensations allowing us to experience the peace of our heart. The voice of the silence within our heart is our divine guide and teacher, opening us to greater and greater possibilities of self-understanding. Silence affects our body through relaxation, our mind through seeing the real from the unreal and our heart through communing with our sacred essence.

Within silence it is possible to have a conscious communion with our source, keeping the flame of our heart burning brightly. When we are plagued with doubt and insecurity we lose our connection with our source and touch into the darkness of this illusionary world. The way to mastery is to turn within to the silence of our true self, the part of us that remains in observation throughout all changes. To live in the light of our true self is to live in stillness where we are unaffected by the changing appearances of manifestation. Through silence of being it is possible to live in the eternal essence of life.

HEALING THROUGH SOUND
SACRED CHANTING AND PRAYER

Om is the word of creation. In the new testament (John, chapter 1 verse 1) it is written, "In the beginning was the word and the word was with God and the word was God." The word referred to is Om.

THE ORIGIN AND NATURE OF SOUND

The root chakra is considered the birthplace of sound within our beings. Sound travels through the chakras as they are awakened and the highest manifestation of sound occurs in the throat center in the form of "Om." In the root center it is expressed as a bird chirping; in the navel center it becomes the twinkling of an anklet; in the solar plexus center it becomes the sound of a bell and then within the heart center it is expressed as the music of a flute. When the cosmic sound or vibration reaches the throat center it manifests as the cosmic sound, *Om.*

The vibration of sound travels along the sushumna channel, cleaning and reenergizing the karmic patterns of the chakras. Sound evolves from the vibration of the Kundalini Shakti that resides in the base center into the navel where it is perceived as rumbling. It moves to the heart and is perceived as un-struck and through the heart to the throat it produces all sounds.

Para is the highest transcendental state, along with pure energy, Shakti – a divine vibration that unites all. Sound is a direct vehicle to access *parashakti,* our highest force.

Sound meditation or *japa* is the art of using sound to transcend consciousness to the highest level of divine expression. The power of sound is a direct way to self-realization, clearing the mind of the clutter of thoughts, emotions and impressions. When the mind is in its natural pure state it reflects the pure consciousness of the infinite.

The use of healing sounds that are expressed with the intention of clearing stagnant energy will bring the higher aspect of truth, divine will and the essence of love and peace into our consciousness. When we use our voice to access divine healing energy through mantras and healing sounds we are able to bring all aspects of our being into alignment with these energies. Through the use of healing sounds we learn to hear intuitively and quicken the development of our higher faculties. Healing sounds are nature's medicine to bring our minds into a state of peace, focus, clarity and attention to the sacred in life.

By the way of the voice we are able to awaken our life force. Our divine consciousness resonates throughout our being and to the beings of the entire world. The awakening of the life force within keeps the mind still and turned inward to the sacred heart.

THE OM SIGN AND ITS SIGNIFICANCE

The Vedas state that creation arises from the first sound of the universe. Aum is the primal sound, which emanated with the first of creation. *A* represents the material universe, the waking state, *U* represents the astral plane – the dreaming state, which includes the emotional and mental aspects of our natural plane and *M* represents the experience that lies above the mind and deep sleep state. Aum signifies the three periods of time, the three states of consciousness and all of existence

The Om (Aum) sound is represented by these symbols: the three is the material world. The dot or *bindu* is the absolute consciousness, encased by the veiling power of mind and body. The crescent sign is the deep sleep subconscious where one holds the knowledge and impressions received from previous incarnations.

The Om sound has three aspects representing Brahma, Vishnu and Shiva. The three aspects also represent the trinity of the God head. These three aspects are embedded in the letters of a, u, m. The sound *a* arises in the throat, the *u* arises from the tongue and *m* arises from the lips; when they join they become Om which arises from the navel. It covers the whole field of the vocal organs, thus Om represents all languages and the world.

The navel is compared to the lotus and is the place where the life force resides. When Om is pronounced it should appear as if a plane is coming from a distance, then drawing closer and closer to us and eventually flying from us. Saying the mantra Om, will rejuvenate the nervous system, bring peace and balance to the body, mind and emotions.

NAMASTE, I SALUTE THE DIVINITY WITHIN YOU

HEALING PRAYERS, SACRED CHANTS

Our prayers are our direct communication with the creator. It is the action of our pure hearts and mind to surrender to divine will and receive guidance.

THE GREAT INVOCATION

From the point of light within the mind of God, let light stream forth into the minds of men. Let light descend on earth. From the point of love within the heart of God, Let love stream forth into the hearts of men. May Christ return to earth.

From the center where the will of God is known, let purpose guide the little wills of people: the purpose which the masters know and serve.

From the center, which we call the race of men, let the plan of love and light work out and may it seal the door where evil dwells.

Let light and love and power restore the plan on earth.

PRAYER OF SAINT FRANCIS

Where there is hatred let me sow love, where there is injury, pardon, where there is despair, let me sow hope, where there is darkness let me sow light. For behold, the kingdom of heaven is within you.

THE LORD'S PRAYER

The Lord's Prayer is useful to all healing and is a great benefit to alignment of the chakras with the soul.

Our father which art in heaven (the crown chakra) hallowed be thy name (the third eye chakra). Thy kingdom come (the crown and head chakra as well as spiritual chakras above the head) thy will be done (the throat chakra) in earth (the root chakra) as it is in heaven (the crown chakra). Give us this day our daily bread (the root, navel and solar plexus chakras) and forgive us our trespasses, (the lower three chakras) as we forgive those who trespass against us (bringing the energy of the earth through the lower chakras transforming it to light and moving the energies through the upper chakras). And lead us not into temptation (the solar plexus chakra) but deliver us from evil (the resurrection of the heart center) for thine is the kingdom (the throat) and the power (the third eye) and the glory, forever, Amen (the crown center).

DIVINE INVOCATIONS

Ask and It will be given to you; seek and you will find; knock, and it will be opened to you. For every one who asks receives, and he who seeks finds, and to him who knocks it will be opened.

Matthew 7:7-8

At the beginning of a healing session an invocation summons guides and creates protection. Here are samples of invocations.

- To the supreme God, thank you for making me thy divine healing instrument. Let my entire being be filled with compassion for others who are suffering.
- To my spiritual teachers, angels and healing guides, thank you for your divine guidance, love and compassion.
- I am created by divine light, I am sustained by divine light, I am protected by divine light, I am surrounded by divine light, I am ever-growing into divine light.

INVOCATIONS TO THE ARCHANGELS

Michael, Angel of protection, a protective force we can call upon, which clears the obstacles of darkness and ignorance, removing the veil from our true identities as beings of light.

Gabriel, Angel of strength, death and resurrection.

Uriel, Angel of communication, messenger of God.

Raphael, Angel of healing.

May Michael be on my right hand, Gabriel on my left, before me, Uriel behind me Raphael and above me the all pervading divine presence.

DIVINE AFFIRMATIONS FOR THE BODY, MIND AND SPIRIT

When working with divine affirmations it is important to find one that supports the evolving nature of the soul. Choosing affirmations appropriate to the moment finds the soul's medicine and assists in the transformation process. Divine affirmations help us release old programming through seeing the consciousness in its perfection of now. Below are some ideas for divine affirmations.

DIVINE AFFIRMATIONS FOR THE BODY

- I am whole, well and in complete balance with the perfection of nature.
- I am radiant, free and full of vitality.
- I completely let go of all imbalances in my system, allowing my body, mind and spirit to be in perfect balance.
- I let go of all memory held in my body, breathing in the present moment free from the past. I see now that my body, mind and spirit are in perfect harmony.
- As I inhale, I focus bringing healing light to my pain and discomfort. As I exhale I let go of all disharmony. I see my self as free from all pain and imbalance.
- I am not this physical body, I am not my emotions or thought. I am eternal and not bound to these conditions.
- I bring space, awareness and light to my life, knowing my nature is infinite, unbounded consciousness.

DIVINE AFFIRMATIONS FOR THE EMOTIONAL AND MENTAL

- I transcend all emotions from my ego nature into the pure emotions of love, light and joy that are expressions of my true self residing in my heart.
- I observe all thoughts that come into my pure consciousness as transient while remaining firmly planted in my heart of purity and stillness.
- My compassion deeply understands the nature of my thoughts and emotions as being scars from identification with my ego self; therefore, I turn all my attention into my heart of sacred wisdom and rest.
- I allow nothing to obscure the vision and oneness of my true nature; all that is temporary simply flows through me and out. I am a sieve of discernment and goodness, loving the divine above all.
- I embody the beauty of the universe, completely letting go of all tendencies to create suffering or pain. I offer my life in service to the divine.
- I let go of all feelings of separation as I merge with my divine consciousness of love and truth.
- I hold my true self dear. I have found a precious rare jewel and keep it safe, polished and radiant at all times.

DIVINE AFFIRMATION FOR THE SPIRIT

- I am one with the divine, offering my life to service and truth.
- The world and its illusion are a stopover for me. My true home is with God. During this stopover I only listen for instructions and obey.
- I offer all of my being to the divine, all that is hidden, all that is revealed. I remain open to divine will, surrendering all personal desires.
- I give myself as a garland of roses to you my Lord, each rose being a lesson learned, each rose with the fragrance of purity and the eternal beauty of my soul.
- I surrender all to the divine, allowing space and emptiness

to meet life's calling. I humbly await the opportunity to serve.
- The past is completely forgiven for I am born anew in the infinite possibilities of my freedom as pure and divine consciousness.
- I let go of all sorrow and memories knowing that my true reality is found in the timelessness of life, where I remain.

HEALING CHANTS, MANTRAS AND SOUNDS

In a spiritual context, the throat center is best used for liberation of the personality self. Through saying mantras, prayer and singing sacred chants we are able to achieve the peace, love and God consciousness that we yearn for.

Mantras are powerful invocations to the divine. They work through the vibration of sound and the intention behind them. Through the practice of turning inward into the stillness of our heart, we begin using a mantra or divine affirmation in support of our soul. When identification shifts from ego self to true divine nature a mantra simply assists the focusing of our mind.

Through the use of a mantra or divine affirmation, we are able to direct attention to our ever-present eternal nature, dissolving any sense of separation, opening to the infinite. The mantra or statement of choice is our vital energy (Shakti) expressed in the form of sound, evoking the divine consciousness within our being.

Many of the mantras suggested in this chapter are derived from the Sanskrit alphabet, the language of the divine. The power of a mantra when applied to a situation will transform the energy, bringing about a change in reality. The correct sound is like an invocation or divine command that sets the vibrations of the cosmos into motion, attracting the requested result.

The throat chakra is considered the chakra of miracles because the voice is able to transcend outer reality through a simple command. For this to occur all the chakras have to be balanced on all levels, specifically the throat. The throat chakra is the center where the voice, when used in relationship to the highest good, can create miracles through commands, prayers and affirmations.

Mantras are very powerful invocations to parashakti, used for the intent to change and transform energy. The vibrations from a mantra will move energy for whatever purpose or intention. To infuse a mantra with power is to activate vibrational channels that produce altered states of consciousness, which aid in remembering our true nature.

THE GAYATRI MANTRA

The Gayatri is the mother of the universe, the supreme Shakti and there is nothing she cannot do. Her mantra purifies the mind, destroys pain, sin and ignorance; brings liberation and bestows health, strength, vitality, power, intelligence and magnetic aura. The Gayatri mantra is the essence of Vedanta that sharpens the intellect.

The Gayatri has three parts: praise, meditation and prayer. First the divine is praised and then meditated upon in reverence and then lastly the appeal is made to the divine to awaken and strengthen the intellect, the discriminating faculty of man.

The Gayatri is the most essential mantra ever known. It is important to recite the Gayatri at least three times a day, morning, noon and evening. The Gayatri dispels the darkness of ignorance and promotes knowledge, wisdom and discrimination. This is a treasure you must guard throughout all of your life. It will protect you from harm, wherever you are. The presence of Brahma will descend on you and illumine your intellect and light your path while this mantra is chanted. Gayatri is the Shakti that animates all life.

GAYATRI ANCIENT MEANING AND PRONUNCIATION

Om (Aum) Symbol of the Para Brahman, the basis of creation.

Bhur (Bhoor) Bhu-Loka, (physical plane) the earth.

Bhuvah (Bhoo- vah) Antariksha-Loka, (astral) atmosphere.

Swah (Sva-ha) Swarga-Loka (celestial plane) absolute substratum of creation, heaven, beyond the causal.

Tat (Taht) Transcendent Para-atman, that ultimate reality.

Savitur - Ishwara or creator, equated with divine power, contained in the sun.

Varenyam - Fit to be worshiped or adored, adore. We adore the glorious power of the pervading sun.

Bargo - Remover of sins and ignorance, glory, radiance.

Devasya - Resplendent, shining from whom all things proceed, divine radiance, grace of God.

Dhemahi - We meditate.

Dhiyo - Buddhic, intellect, understanding, May he enlighten our intellects, (prayer).

Yo - Which, who

Nah - Our

Prachodayat - Enlighten, guide, impel. May the prayer direct our intellect towards ultimate reality.

(Dhiyo-Yo-Nat Pracho-dayatt)

THE MANTRA

Om (O Thou) Bhur (physical) Bhuvah (astral) Svah (celestial) Tat (the transcendent) Savitur (the creator) Varenyam (fit to be worshipped) Bhargo (remover of ignorance, return to glory) Devasya (shining) Dheemahe (we the universe) Dhiyo (understanding) Yo (which, who) Nah (our) Prachodayat (enlighten, guide, impel).

Who givest sustenance to and to whom all things return, unveil to us the face of the true spiritual sun hidden by a disc of golden light. That we may know the truth and do our whole duty, as we journey to thy sacred feet. Oh God, thou are the giver of life, the remover of pain and sorrow, the bestower of happiness. Oh, creator of the universe, may we receive sin-destroying light. Om.

OM SHANTI, OM SHANTI, OM SHANTI OM, OM SHANTI, OM SHANTI, OM
The great peace mantra.

OM MANE PADME HUM (AA-OO-M MAH-NEE-PAD-MAY HOOM)
Om, jewel in the lotus, Hum - Harmonizes nerve tissues, clears subtle impurities from the nadis and nerves, empowers all actions on the subtle level, infusing the cosmic life force into the healing process. Male and female energies come into balance.

OM NAMAH SHIVAYA, OM NAMAH SHIVAYA, OM NAMAH SHIVAYA, SHIVAYAH NAMAH OM
Shiva, lord of ascetics and recluses, is part of the Hindu trinity. Brahma and Vishnu, the other two parts, are associated with creation and preservation. Shiva, the cosmic dancer, presides over the destructive energies, which break up the universe at the end of each age. This is the process of the old making way for the new; in a more personal sense, "I honor the divine within."

HARE OM, HARE OM, HARE HARE OM, HARE OM, HARE OM, HARE HARE OM
Hare is another name for Vishnu. The aspect which forgives the past actions of those who take refuge in him and destroys their negative deeds. Hare is a redeemer and a guide to personal salvation as well as the world preserver.

HARE RAMA, HARE RAMA, RAMA RAMA, HARE HARE, HARE RAMA, HARE RAMA, HARE HARE, HARE KRISHNA, HARE KRISHNA, KRISHNA KRISHNA, HARE HARE
Hare is the glorified form of address for calling upon God. Rama and Krishna were two of the best-known and most beloved incarnations of Vishnu. They took human birth on this earth to lead mankind to eternal salvation. This is the maha mantra, the easiest and surest way for attaining God realization in this present age.

OM SRI RAM JAI RAM, JAI JAI RAM OM SRI RAM JAI RAM JAI JAI RAM
Victory to Rama, Jaya means victory.

GATE GATE, PARAGATE PARASAMGATE, BODHISVAHA
Meaning "Gone, gone, beyond all illusions of the physical plane, on the breath."

HEALING SOUNDS
SOUND/PRONUNCIATION/ MEANING AND BENEFITS.

Aum / Om - (home) the divine word serving to energize or empower all things, good for the spine and restores and energizes the entire body and mind. Awakens prana, opens channels, all mantras begin and end with Om. Clears the mind and increases the strength of our immune system. Awakens prana of positive energy and healing.

Ram - (a sounds like a in calm) Brings in divine protection (light and peace) giving strength, calm, rest, peace, good for mental disorders, such as insomnia, bad dreams, nervousness, anxiety, excessive fear and fright, helps build the immune system.

Hoom - Wards off negative influences, which manifest as diseases, negative emotions, awakens the agni and promotes digestive fire.

Aym - (i-eem) Improves mental concentration, thinking, rational powers and speech, awakens and increases intelligence, mental and nervous disorders. Restores speech, communication, control of the senses, mind and is the sacred sound of the Goddess of wisdom, Saraswati.

Shrim - Promotes general health, beauty, creativity, prosperity; strengthens overall health and harmony.

Krim - Gives capacity for work and actions, adds power and efficacy, good for chanting while making preparations.

Hrim - As in seem. Cleanses and purifies, giving energy, joy and ecstasy, although it initially causes atonement; throat, palate, nose, respiratory, digestive.

Hraim - (hah-reem) Time, kidney.

Hra - Hurrah, continuous long a, strengthens the rib cage, purifies the alimentary canal.

Hram - (hraaaammm) as in calm. Restorative for lungs, asthma.

Hrum - The long vowel u is pronounced in rhyme with room, stimulates liver, spleen, stomach and reduces abdomen.

Sham - Mantra of peace. Creates calmness, detachment, contentment, alleviates mental and nervous disorders, stress, anxiety, disturbed emotions, tremors, shaking, nervous system disorders.

Shum - (pronounced like shoe but shorter vowel sound) Increases vitality, energy, fertility.

Som - As in home. Increases energy, vitality, joy, delight, creativity, strengthens mind, heart, nerves; is good for rejuvenation and notification.

Ram - Brings in divine protection, light and grace giving strength and calm, rest and peace; good for mental disorders, builds immune system.

A Hoom - Wards off negative influences, diseases, negative emotions, awakens agni, wisdom, increases digestive fire and clears channels; increases mental perception.

PEACE PRAYER

Lord, make me an instrument of your peace
Where there is hatred, let me bring love
Where there is injury, pardon
Where there is doubting, let me bring faith
And Lord, make me an instrument of your peace,
Where there is despairing let me bring hope,
Where there is darkness, light
Where there is sadness, let me bring joy
Oh Divine Master, grant that I might seek
Not so much to be consoled as to console
To be understood, as to understand
Not so much to be loved, as to love another
For it is in giving that we now receive
It is in pardoning that we are now pardoned,

John Michael Talbot

THE THROAT CHAKRA CHART

Visuddha - Meaning purification, simplified, sanctified, free from doubt. The chakra of miracles.

Location - Between collarbones, third cervical vertebrae, base of neck

Physical Correspondence - Throat, neck, thyroid, parathyroid, ears, mouth, teeth

Physical Dysfunctions - Sore throats, colds, swollen glands, neck pain, dental problems, thyroid problems, asthma, hearing or ear problems

Glandular Connection - Thyroid and parathyroid - controls jaw, neck, throat, voice, airways, upper lungs, nape of neck, arms

Emotional Plane - Inability to express emotions, blocked creativity, transformation of feelings and emotions, communication, reflections

Mental Plane - Blocked flow of creative expression by thought and self-doubt; thought and mind create negativity about self and block ability to express emotions; low self-esteem due to thought and conditioning

Color - Bright blue expression, light blue the quality of truth

Petals - 16

Element - Ether

Symbol - Lotus with 16 petals, containing a downward pointing triangle within a circle representing the full moon

Subtle Body - Buddhic

Sense - Hearing

Fragrance - Sage, eucalyptus, frankincense, lavender, sandalwood, chamomile, myrrh

Ayurvedic Oils - Sandalwood, tea tree

Healing Stones - Aquamarine, turquoise, chalcedony, lapis lazuli, agate, celestite, sodalite, sapphire

Sounds - EEE

Mantras - HAM

Animal Symbol - Elephant holding one of his seven trunks up in the air victoriously

Words to Create Healing Affirmations - Express, self, listen, be truthful, voice, power, affirm, command, commune, allow, harmony in expression, harmlessness, wishes, invoke, prayer, communication, perfect, creative, ask, miracles, sanctify

Actions - I speak, I bring forth, I ask, I allow, I open

Yoga Postures - Neck Rolls, Fish Pose, Shoulder Stand, The Plough, Head Lift, Salutation to the Sun

Balanced Center: We express our thoughts, feelings and emotions with inner knowing and without fear. We allow ourselves to be honest with others and ourselves. Speech is clear, reflecting inner truth. Silence is easily practiced from conviction in our truth. We remain true to ourselves and can say both yes and no to life, when we follow our heart. We are not swayed by others opinions. We are in contact with our inner guide, giving spaciousness to our being.

Unbalanced Center: Sometimes we will express ourselves in thoughtless actions or shut ourselves off from our feelings of truth. We sometimes carry a feeling of judgment of others and ourselves. When unbalanced our voice is comparatively loud and our words lack inner meaning. Through being unbalanced in this center we can act defensively and use words harshly to hurt others. Sometimes there is a tendency to manipulate others. Insufficient energy in the throat chakra can express itself in shyness, being overly quiet and getting a lump in the throat when needing to speak.

THIRD EYE CHAKRA MEDITATION

Your journey takes you into the creative realm of spirit, the home of unlimited potential. Within your inner eye you see clearly the vision of your unbounded self. Your inner eye is the eye of light, transforming all darkness into light, all fear into love. Through seeing, accepting and embracing you return to the essence of creative power. Turn within and allow the radiant light of spirit to walk you down the middle path, merging all opposites into the oneness of God. This is your sacred path leading you to the silence of your true nature.

AFFIRMATION OF CELESTIAL PERCEPTION
I close my outer eyes and turn within to see
the truth of my life and I allow God's grace
to appear before me.

Chapter Seventeen

THE THIRD EYE CENTER
SHIELD OF THE INTUITIVE PLANE

If Thine eye be single thy whole body
shall be full of light
Luke 11:34

Located between the eyebrows, the ajna center or the eye of wisdom is the center of our higher intuition. *Ajna* means to perceive in Sanskrit. The ajna is related to the crown chakra, reflecting the light of the atmic plane of consciousness. Our sixth sense or clair-voyance (clear seeing) is developed in the third eye chakra where we attain an inner sense of knowing and live in the magic and pos-sibilities of our life. The related endocrine gland is the pituitary gland, which is said to be the seat of the soul.

The sixth chakra is the master center for the centers below and has the gift of will and the power of visualization. The third eye chakra being the command center for all the other centers makes it vitally important that we open to its full potential in our lifetime. This is accomplished through quieting the mind, deep contemplation and inquiry into the nature of the true self. When this center is fully awak-ened it has the power to transform all conditions of our life, releas-ing karmic patterns from the past and healing our body, mind and emotions.

As stated earlier, Shiva resides in the crown center and Shakti resides in the root center. Within the third eye they meet and unify, creating a marriage of heaven and earth. The ajna center is the center where the ida, pingala and sushumna nadis merge to form a single passageway to the crown center.

The third eye center, when awakened, illuminates the path of return to the radiant light of spirit. The symbol of this center is two wings with the Om sign in the middle indicating freedom from the pairs of opposites. Through the opening of the third eye we develop inner seeing - the art of inquiry into the truth of our being. As we deepen the awakening of the ajna center we realize the non-dual nature of our true reality, which expresses itself as peace and calmness regardless of the changing experiences of our life. From this center we learn to walk the middle path through the eye of the needle — the point between all opposites.

This sixth chakra opens us to deeper levels of perception and balance where the energy of matter and spirit become one. We find a deep peace within our inner eye when we close our outer eyes. Meditation becomes a vehicle to rest in the light of our pure consciousness just as sleep is necessary for rest of our physical body.

The third eye center opens when the love of the heart surges upward awakening the wisdom and will of the divine centers. Through our developed inner vision we connect with the immortal triad of our soul, the love, wisdom and will aspects of our true self. This great triangle of divine energies then becomes the directing force of our life.

As we realize our true nature we develop the strength necessary to navigate the passage through life with great skill. When we merge the energies of light and love together we create a powerful healing force, which clears the path for selfless service. Service that lets go of self-inflicted suffering and sees what needs to be done to help those truly in need.

The saying "be in the world but not of it" is appropriate for the development of the ajna center as we learn to shift our attention from the world of change to the changeless essence of the divine. We awaken our inner eye through quiet contemplation, asking ourselves the most important question that points us to our true nature.

This question, "Who am I?" leads us safely to the essence of our true self.

The wisdom eye is the window to our radiant true nature and when opened it gives us insight to our divine purpose. This window reflects the light of the soul, the realm of our higher knowledge. Our divine purpose is found through letting go of the conditioning from the past and the thought of who we think we are based on time and memory. This divine action frees us to discover the eternal presence within our hearts.

The ajna center is a place of celestial perception where it is possible to perceive the subtle energies of a nonphysical realm. On an emotional level it is how we see that determines our experience. An example is a rope lying on the ground being mistaken for a snake. Our hearts might stop in fear over something that wasn't real. Reality is based on our beliefs and judgments. On a mental level the balanced ajna center can offer a sense of being open and receptive to the world, allowing emotions to flow and our higher intuition to be our guiding force.

The third eye represents the energy where duality has merged into one unified consciousness. It is through our developing awareness of our true self that we transcend and merge all sense of separation into the unifying force of the sacred.

SELF INQUIRY FOR THE WISDOM CENTER

Through a journal or meditation ask questions:

Question Reality

The game your mind creates and then plays along with.

Question Existence

When the beginning creates the end and the end is just another beginning.

Question Life

A gift from an unknown source.

Question Truth

The truth of what and who your are.

You are the creator of your own reality, existence, life and truth. Whether love or fear based, these are the seeds of all manifestation.

It is your duty to be that which you are and to understand that which has no past, no future. It is now and always in a space of timeless being, free from birth and death, free from reality, existence, life. It is that which forever holds you and that which you forever hold, the creator, the destroyer, the infinite preserver. It forever is and holds stillness and silence, it is beyond the highest feeling of love and light but is the pure essence of it.

Question Everything.

JOURNEY THROUGH THE CHAKRAS COLOR MEDITATION

Relax and allow your breath to assist in releasing tensions, worries and anxieties. Feel yourself letting go into a deeper and deeper state of peace. Breathe gently from your lower abdomen. Slowly, deeply, your breath moves throughout your being assisting you in relaxation. Let your awareness move to your lower abdomen; the base of the spine where the seat of the root chakra and the Kundalini reside. This is your grounding center, the foundation of your being. Feel a sense of belonging, inner security and trust, knowing that you are on a grand journey of life to the kingdom of your own divinity. Your purpose here is to trust, accept and learn the art of being. You have inner security and gratitude for the opportunity this birth brings. Visualize a glowing red sun here, nurturing and awakening your vital force within. Feel the vital energy of the earth as it enters the root chakra intensely connecting you with the earth. Feel grounded and centered, let go of any insecurity within the sacred life force.

As your breathing comes into rhythm with the vital energy running up your spine, feel your awareness move to the sacral center; the center of cleansing water that circulates around your abdominal area, cleansing, refreshing and purifying physical and emotional toxins. Bring a golden-orange ray of vital energy here, allow your physical creative force to surface, embrace your passion for life and feel the miracle of the vital force within you.

As you move from the watery, creative substance of the second chakra into the fiery nature of the third, the solar plexus chakra, you feel alive with the flowing, vital current of your being. Embrace your sense of self and feel secure in life's process. Now allow your awareness to enter the fiery solar plexus region, the physical sun of your universe. This is the source of personal power, the chakra of transformation. As you move your awareness from personal identification to your true nature of the impersonal self feel the glowing energy here. The golden color of the solar plexus center warms your entire being. Your breath takes you into deeper relaxation and ease as you allow all worries and concerns to melt in the warmth, bringing a deep sense of peace, strength and abundance.

Know that through the breath you can relax and bring calmness and healing light to all thoughts and emotions. You are in the center of your radiance. Allow the personal self to transcend its own sense of power to the power of divine will. This requires a surrender of identification held in separation; know that you are one unified whole in union with the divine nature of your being.

Move from the flaming sea of the solar plexus to the gentle harmlessness of the heart center, sensing your integration with light. There is a beautiful color of rose pink here representing unconditional love and a hue of green representing the healing light of the soul. You feel the love and compassion deep within your heart.

Bring this awareness of your true nature as you enter the throat chakra. The miracle of this center is knowing and expressing your truth so that all things beautiful and true in your life are manifest. Feel a light blue radiance here, as you open to the unlimited expansion of perception and divine creativity. Allow yourself to discern the truth, express the truth and listen within to the infinite space and unbounded consciousness of your divine essence. The radiance of this center opens you to deeper levels of truth and you move into the ajna center, the eye of wisdom and stillness, where you access unlimited perception and understanding of life.

This wisdom center, bathed in indigo light, takes you to the infinite creation. You feel receptive and at peace with all of life as you penetrate the stillness of empty space. Thoughts dissipate in this stillness as you connect with the sacred force. The journey has taken you into the realm of cosmic knowledge, beyond all concepts and thoughts. This silence carries you to the home of your true self; you now go into the integration force of the crown chakra.

A brilliant purple light floods down through all your chakras, integrating and bringing their energies into balance. You feel unleashed from all chains of temporary manifestation; you have moved into the eternal, free flowing energy of the unbounded consciousness of the crown chakra. You have now merged all sense of separation into the omnipresent and radiant light of God.

THE THIRD EYE CHAKRA

Ajna - Meaning servant, or ordered from above, not ignorant, ocean of nectar
Location - First cervical vertebra, center of the Head at the eye level or slightly above.
Physical Correspondence - Pituitary gland, left lower brain, left eye, ears, nose, nervous system
Physical Dysfunctions - Headaches, poor vision, eye problems, nightmares
Glandular Connection - Pituitary - controls endocrine system
Emotional Plane - Lack of ability to integrate feelings with wisdom, learning difficulties, hallucinations, how we see determines our experience.
Mental Plane - Thoughts and conditioning mind block clear perception.
Spiritual Plane - Extrasensory perception, knowledge of being
Subtle Body - Intuitional
Color - Indigo
Petals - 2 associated with hemispheres, left - analytical, logical, mathematical and linear, right - spatial, artistic, intuitive and holistic
Element - Ether, light and telepathic energy
Symbol - Lotus with 2 large petals on either side, resembling wings, around a circle containing a downward pointing triangle.
Sense - Sixth sense, light
Fragrance - Mint, jasmine, violet, rose, lotus, geranium, rosemary, basil
Ayurvedic Oils - Sandalwood, basil, lavender, jasmine, eucalyptus
Healing Stones - Lapis lazuli, blue sapphire, sodalite, quartz, opal
Sounds - Vowels: sound therapy vowel sound E sung in A
Mantras - KSHAM
Words to Create Healing Affirmations - Understanding, harmony, oneness, knowing, intuiting, light, seeing, awareness, vision, recognize, inner truth, trust, divine plan, imagination, visualization, clarity, purpose, willingness, servant, light
Action Verb - I see, I am, I create, I ask, I command,
Yoga Postures - Palming the eyes
Balanced Center: Means living in harmony with divine law, no longer manipulating life with self-interest. Celestial perception becomes our second nature, using thought from the intellect as tools to employ a divine life style. There is no longer a sense of duality as this center when fully awakened expresses the middle path of equilibrium, and the inherent unity of life. We attain the gift of visualization and the ability to comprehend life intuitively. We are open to cosmic truths and see the world of appearances as temporary illusions and do not get caught up in them. Our thoughts are vehicles of reality and are used for the purpose of divine order and work. We learn to perceive the world in a different way, noticing the grace of life with ever deepening awareness. We become intuitive, ever opening and unfolding to the divine aspects of reality. Joyous communication, untouched by fear, self preserved and protected.
Unbalanced Center: Overly intellectual, overly rational, lacking a holistic way of thinking, an inability to integrate. We block the light of our vision with our conditioned thought. We sometimes are not able to integrate the experience that we have had in our changing life, as well as we lose perception of reality. Our ideas are based on concrete thinking and we have not developed the ability to move beyond rational thought into perception. We have suppressed our feelings and live in dependency of others will.

The mind shines not by its own light. It is not self-luminous. It borrows its light from consciousness from which it springs. It is like a moon, which reflects the sun's light.

Sri Nisargatta Maharaj

Chapter Eighteen

THE CROWN CENTER

SHIELD OF THE DIVINE PLANE

*We are all one self - the self of pure awareness. This self, this flawless
awareness is God. There is only God.*

Ashatavakra Gita

There is no duality in the Turiya state: everything has merged in the Self.

Adi Shankaracharya

The *sahasrara* chakra, meaning thousandfold in Sanskrit, is
located on the top of the head at the baby's soft spot. This exquisite
white thousand-petaled lotus forms a most beautiful crown on the
head with the stem or antahkarana reaching upward as a channel
for divine energies. It is the soul's point of entry and exit as well as
a receiving and distributing station for our life force. It is most acti-
vated through yearning to unite with our God selves as well as the
inquiry into the sacred nature of life.

The channel between the personality and the higher consciousness of being must be purified to allow the continuous inflow of divine energy, which brings us the gifts of wisdom, power and love.
We must recognize that our lower vehicles which are based on survival, reproduction, desires, self-importance, fear, anger, greed, etc.
have directed our way of thinking in an uncontrolled and chaotic
manner. Impressions of this suffering are left in our subconscious
mind and color our life, our true self and our relationship to the world.

These scars and impressions are called *samskaras* in Sanskrit.

Opening the crown center allows the divine to clear the past impressions, creating an unconditional relationship to life based on the present. Jesus said, "Empty thyself and I shall fill thee" which implies a divine energy entering through the crown. It is when we empty ourselves of the scars and conditioning of the past that we are born anew into the light of our true consciousness. This center is greatly affected when we live a life of service, meditation and aspire to know our true self.

The crown chakra is a center for universal consciousness with the duty of integrating and synthesizing all energies into one unified whole. The seventh chakra connects us with cosmic consciousness. The energy that is poured through the crown is very purifying and unifies us with our life's purpose. The channel widens as our consciousness expands taking us deeper into our unknown mysterious nature.

The root chakra being at the base of the sushumna channel is directly linked with the divine energies of the crown. When the root and crown are in balance we have access to our full human potential and life force. The root center being the consciousness of the material life and the crown being the consciousness of the spiritual life, allow us to walk the middle path of which the Buddha spoke. Through the balancing of these two forces we build a foundation of trust and security; we touch into the timelessness of life.

The crown center is related to the pineal gland where the thread of consciousness is anchored connecting us with our soul. The seventh chakra is an organ of synthesis of great beauty, the center where the will, creativity and consciousness are integrated. It unifies the beauty of the heart center, the truth of the throat center and the goodness of the third eye center. Through our ascension process we develop a closer connection with our true self each step of the way.

The crown center holds the essence of divine grace and is opened through silence, purity and meditative prayer. The energy received from this center moves down through the spinal column unifying, healing and balancing our body, mind and spirit. The centers along the spine come into full expression when all negative conditions are released.

We have journeyed on the path of return through our energy anatomy from the personality aspects of our being to our sacred souls. We have learned to honor our humanity and live in each sacred moment cherishing the vehicles of our expression. The crown center invites us to integrate, synthesize and unify all our life experiences. It teaches us to reach beyond the chattering thought of our conditioned mind into the infinite beauty of our creator.

THE ART OF MEDITATION

Empty yourself of everything, Let the mind become still. The ten thousand things rise and fall while the self watches their return. The returning to the source is stillness, which is the way of nature.

Lao Tsu, Tao Te Ching

Meditation is a state of communion with the divine - the pure essence of God within our heart. Through turning within to the silence of our true nature meditation becomes a natural act of union with our sacred self. The beginning of meditation is through knowing our true nature. There cannot be true meditation unless we know who is it that is meditating. The ego that is identified with self will only meditate to gain something. Through knowing our true nature it is possible for true meditation to take place.

By quieting the mind, we become a witness to its game, understanding the nature of its restlessness. We see clearly that our separate sense of self is formed through the belief in the thoughts of the mind with its accompanying emotions. The knowledge of our true self gives us the inner strength and courage to turn the mind back to its source and dissolve the false accumulation of thought. This gives space for the mind to be born anew and be purified from the past, leading ultimately to peace and freedom of being. When the mind is at peace there is a clarity and divine force that enables us to make responsible decisions in a peaceful and calm manner.

When the mind dissolves into the heart of stillness it is possible to see the divine in all of creation. There is no longer a sense of a separate self believing in the thoughts that display as the essential truth. Meditation is the natural state of the self that has turned inward and rests in the light of the heart. Through deep inner silence, we experience a unity in life, where all is laid to rest in the peace of the sacred force that is always present.

Meditation and quieting the mind are essential tools to access the true self that resides within. The outward pursuit of the mind to acquire things for happiness is a trap that most humans find themselves in for a lifetime.

The mind is the content of our experiences, the sum total of our thoughts and emotions creating our ego identification. When the mind is allowed to function without restraint it will go to any length to reproduce the past and create the future based on comparison and judgment.

Samskaras (scarring or impression) are impressions that are formed in the mind from past experiences. These impressions are the ebb and flow of thought waves. They create deep grooves of suffering through identification with the false nature of life. Through the process of quieting the mind and turning it back into its source within the heart we can release these impressions from the past, thereby returning to our natural state of peace and stillness. As we release the hold of the mind and sink deeply into our true nature meditation becomes a communion with the sacred. This sacred force infuses our entire being with its purifying and healing light.

The yearning to be free from personal suffering and to unite with our God self must be our intention for any lasting results in meditation. We must discern the habit of the mind to indulge in patterns of suffering and sorrow through its negative programming, stopping the endless habit of personal suffering.

Our identification with our ego self brings us a deep sense of separation and duality, the obstacle to peace and tranquility with our true self. We become bound to the chattering mind and the constant fluctuations of the mind of duality. This duality is the source of seeking that which is pleasurable and running away from that which is painful.

Through the quiet mind and its natural meditative state we learn to access the divine energy of our being, parashakti. This force will guide, inspire, encourage and bring a positive energy to whatever we need in life. The source of parashakti is within, revealed by simply calling it forth to use for healing and for aligning ourselves with a greater light.

We learn to discern between the mind that is outward bound with its habit of constantly searching, never satisfied and our inward reality – our true self. We see that the mind's activity of craving, wanting and desiring take us away from our true nature of rest and peace. When the mind is turned inward it goes into the depth of its own mysterious nature, deepening into its natural state of silence. When turned outward the qualities of our lower nature are nourished and take control; we lose ourselves in the wilderness of the un-contained ego.

When we are vigilant about remaining faithful to our inner nature, we remain in the moment where the mind has no power of projection. Through concentration and attention we can keep the mind steady for the task at hand and bring it home to rest in the heart. The source of intelligence is found through this rest, where all activity is born.

In life we live as though we are puppets on a string with the mind in control. We are slaves to all its desires. Through this activity we lose touch with our true nature, which is, in reality, the master of the mind. When we practice the art of meditation we have the opportunity to disengage ourselves from the grip of the mind and reverse the order of control. We have to see clearly that the old commands of the mind based on the thoughts and desires of the ego self are no longer appropriate. These old commands have taken up the sacred spaces in our life, creating real energies that we follow blindly.

Through stillness of the mind we begin the meditation process with our true self and experience the vastness of our energy that is free from thought. The sacred found within is free from passing thoughts and emotions; something far more magical and mystical than could ever be conjured up by the mind.

Our true nature lives in each moment, is reborn in the next moment and is constantly dying to the old. This renewal process of each moment requires us to practice letting go through our breath. On each inhalation we affirm the new and on the exhalation we let go of the old. We learn to value our true self, above all remaining faithful to the sacred in life. When thoughts come up we can learn to just observe; remaining at rest and in complete stillness within the seat of our heart.

We must learn the art of stopping and being with the moment. This is the most necessary action for one who desires freedom from the ego self. True greatness requires the strength to stop and allow our beings the space needed for life's revelation.

True meditation is the point of silence where all activity of the mind dissolves and the light of the divine is revealed. We cherish this light as a most precious delicate force, quietly abiding in its presence, ever faithful to the holy energy encountered.

REFLECTIONS ON THE NOBLE EIGHTFOLD PATH

Buddha brought to your world eight great truths to guide you on the path of return. The noble eightfold path is a creed or sacred contract that teaches you how to walk in the light of your true self with the intention of ending suffering for humanity.

RIGHT SEEING

Live in remembrance of your soul's essence. See the world without illusion; see clearly the facts of life, what is. When you live in the moment you are able to view life without the conditioning of the past. See all with an awakened eye allowing the mind to cling to nothing and be born anew each day. Your awakened being sees the beauty of each moment holding nothing. When you let go of attachment to ideas, concepts, thoughts, images and impressions you find freedom and discover an unconditional relationship to life.

RIGHT INTENTION

Your intention is to find freedom from personal sorrow. This is your birthright, a life of happiness and goodness. Let go of self-deception and the negative effects of the false identification with the personality. Use your will for the highest good, learn to live with compassion for this suffering world, offering loving kindness to all sentient beings. Connect your mind with your heart; realize that the highest intelligence can be gained through the blending of love and wisdom. Look at how the search for pleasure brings pain and pain again brings the search for pleasure. Have the intention to stop personal self-inflicted suffering. Live in acceptance of self and others with the prayer for happiness for all suffering beings.

RIGHT SPEECH

Learn to speak the truth and express your Buddhic nature. Tell no lies; use words to help or assist learning. Speak kindly and with harmlessness. Speak from your true nature, from the heart of your being. Through prayer you commune with the sacred presence within your heart. A great joy comes through silence.

RIGHT ACTION

When you practice and honor your intention for freedom, you naturally employ right action. Live in the light of harmlessness with the intention of not hurting any life form. Harmlessness is the teaching that employs right action. You become a gentle being with compassion for others and yourself. Live in the light of service; reach into your heart for a spirit of generosity and goodness.

RIGHT LIVELIHOOD

Living in your truth will lead you to do what you love, causing no harm to others and increasing your integrity through your abundant nature. You see that all expressions should be in support of your spirit, honoring and caring for the things most important in life. Await life's call for service.

RIGHT EFFORT

The intention for freedom of being is the foundation for all practice. Realizing your true nature is the first step in this intention. Living with inspiration from your divine nature and following its guidance will lead you to unconditional happiness and love. Find time for the mind to retreat in silence; commune with the healing force of nature.

RIGHT MINDFULNESS

Through your awakening process you will learn to let go of the past that was identified with the false nature of the self. Memories of the past based on false identification do not exist; they are records of illusions that need to be released. Relaxing into your true nature of peace you know that you are, in truth, an untouched being free from all scars of the past. Awareness of your true being leads you to lasting healing of your body, mind and spirit. Through releasing the past you allow yourself to be fully present in the now. Stop all activity of the mind that is geared toward memory and allow the meeting of the true self found in the eternal present.

RIGHT ATTENTION

Surrender all doubt that stems from thought that wanders in and out of consciousness. Train the mind to become focused in the center of being, acquiring stillness and one-pointedness. Forget all that has been acquired through false identification and yet live in remembrance of your true sacred essence. Meditation is simply the surrendering of all holdings, facing the emptiness of being and breathing in your true nature

SHAMBALLA AND OUR GUIDING LIGHT

In our final stages of evolution, we come into contact with the realm of the highest creative expression of divinity available to our being, *Shamballa*, the planetary ruler. Shamballa is a center of consciousness that synthesizes and purifies the lower planes in order to open the pathway for beings to ascend to this higher plane; its sole purpose is to carry out divine will.

The great body of Shamballa is the house of God, composed of spiritual beings that are working in harmony with the aspects of love, wisdom and power. This divine energy is periodically released on the planet as radiant beams of light, resulting in magnificent creativity as well as an evolution of higher values.

Through the quiet mind we can access a guiding light that protects, assists and guides us in becoming divine human beings. Our guiding light instructs and inspires us to move through the identification with lower vehicles of the body, mind and emotions into the higher vehicles of our soul's wisdom. When we connect with this light we are led through gateways of our limitations into our unlimited sacred nature. This requires letting go of the illusion of who we think we are based on memory, time and conditioning. Our surrendering leads us to the temple of our heart, which is full of glory, eternal joy, peace and rest. The gateway to this temple asks that we leave the burdens that we carry from our past identification on its doorstep.

We are a divine spark of our creator, the source of all light, love and wisdom. Through our connection with our source we receive guidance and comfort during the arduous journey of physical existence. When we dissolve the sense of separation created through false identification we become open to receive the transmissions of light. The light within comes to us through our greatest aspirations of beauty, peace and joy found when our mind and heart are unified in stillness. As we become a soul-infused personality, the next door of the path opens. It is the door of the inner ashram to the temple of our soul.

Our soul is the connecting link between the creator and our

personality. Through the harmony and union of our soul with our personality it is possible to live a life of great joy, beauty and peace. It is through divine understanding, when the mind is held steadily in the light, that we are able to contact Shamballa. This force is steadily creating the will of good, annihilating the will of evil.

The average person has not discovered his or her true self, therefore the journey is long and arduous, taking many incarnations to even touch the higher self and beyond. Masters and avatars are synchronized with Shamballa and work to fulfill the divine will of God. It is through the evolution of the personality that one attains contact with the forces of Shamballa.

RADIANT LIGHT MEDIATION

Your luminous body is your eternal nature, a radiant circle of light that surrounds your being. This is your vehicle of light, where you touch into the sacred healing energy of the infinite. Allow yourself to move beyond the confinements of the personality into the realm of your celestial body, which links you to the universal source of unbounded consciousness. You are, in essence, this unbounded consciousness, free from the temporary conditions of manifestation. Formless and unrestricted by time and space, allow your being to soar into the realm of the omnipresent force of life. In your light body, all sheaths are removed and you are infinitely free. Expand into this plane of celestial magnificence, where you are with the eternal, vast nature of the essence of life, the sacred, formless consciousness of being.

SANSKRIT PRAYER
From the unreal, lead me to the real.
From darkness lead me into the light.
From death lead me into immortality.
Om Shanti, Shanti, Shanti. Peace, Peace, Peace.

THE CROWN CHAKRA CHART

Sahasrara - Meaning granting victory, producing might, possessing one thousand petaled lotus, or immortal self.

Location - Top and center of the head, the baby's soft spot

Soul Lesson - Unity, integration

Physical Correspondence - Pituitary, pineal gland, upper brain, right eye, central nervous system

Physical Dysfunctions - Immune system, circulation, endocrine disorders

Glandular Connection - Pineal. Controls cerebrum, right brain hemisphere, central nervous system, right eye

Emotional Plane - Depression, obsession, confusion, hopelessness, disassociation, ungrounded. When the seventh chakra is closed the accumulated wisdom and lessons of the soul remain unconscious. The open seventh chakra becomes the channel of communication to the higher self.

Mental Plane - The chatter of the mind becomes unbearable, psychotic, thoughts that create anxiety, frustration, and fear.

Subtle Body - Divine

Color - Gold, white or violet

Petals - 1000

Element - All elements, thought, cosmic energy

Symbol - A 1000 petaled lotus flower

Sense - Beyond self, thought

Fragrance - Lavender, frankincense, lotus, rosewood, spruce, olibanum

Ayurvedic Oils - Sandalwood, frankincense, myrrh

Healing stones - Amethyst, clear quartz, diamond, crystal, topaz, alexandrite, sapphire, selenite

Sounds or Mantras - Om

Words to create healing affirmations - I am, limitation, universe, connections, spirit, channel, open, radiant, choose, transform, release, surrender, open, I am that, contentment, being, transform

Verbs - I know, I am, I now, I realize

Yoga postures - Half lotus, head stand, meditation

Balanced Center - We have journeyed from our expression as separate individuals and have integrated all our experiences and gifts. Now we experience life as a divine inner child and remember the magical journey of our childlike nature. We can see that we are the same energy that flows in all aspects of life; we are the wind and the sea. Through the development of this center we are balanced with our earth energies and can access our subconscious feelings.

Unbalanced Center - Our thoughts and emotions are still holding onto identification with our lower self, we feel frustrated at our inability to let go. Our power is suppressed in the lower self-holding onto time, memory and the past. We often experience depression and feel out of touch with life.

GLOSSARY

Abhaya - fearlessness, one of the most important virtues, the fruit of knowing one's true nature.

Abhaya mudra - hand position to dispel fear, fingers on the right hand raised, palms facing forward, gesture of protection.

Absolute - ultimate reality

Advaita - non-dual

Advidya - ignorance

Agni - the fire god

Ahamkara - personal ego

Ahimsa - nonviolent path, harmlessness

Ajna - the sixth chakra or third eye, located between the eyebrows.

Akasha - space

Akashic records - the records held within the causal body of the soul.

Anahata - fourth chakra meaning unstruck, located in the heart center.

Ananda - bliss

Anandamaya - the subtlest bliss formed sheath of the causal body. The sphere of all transcendent, blissful consciousness.

Ananta - endless

Antahkarana - the building of the ego instrument or bridge between lower manas (mind) and higher manas. "That path which lies between thy spirit and thy self."

Apana - the prana, which carries away the waste products from the human body.

Arupa - literally without form; that is, a form from the standpoint of the physical plane.

Asmita - egoism (I am that)

Astral body - the subtle body containing prana, mind, intellect and emotions.

Atman - the self; the divine aspect in the seven fold constitution of man; his highest principle.

Aum - the sacred three-syllable word of mantric significance, it is at once an invocation, a benediction, an affirmation and a promise.

Aura - literally means breeze - the vital force surrounding the body.

Awareness - individual consciousness, knowing, witness, perception.

Being - pure consciousness, essential divine nature, changeless, formless, existence.

Bhagavad Gita - the divine song.

Bhajans - singing of religious songs.

Bhakti - devotion

Bhava - becoming

Blessings - the unseen grace of life, not conditioned upon good or bad but on events to open one up to divine reality.

Brahma - the creator

Bridge of light - antahkarana

Buddha - the enlightened one

Buddhi - intellect

Causal body - the subtlest of the three bodies, also known as the seed body. Contains the karmic imprint that determines who you are.

Causal plane - the highest plane of manifestation.

Celestial - heavenly region of divine beings.

Chakra - the astral force centers or spiritual center located in the Sushumna, literally meaning disk or wheel.

Chin mudra - hand position of joined thumb and index finger.

Clairvoyance - clear seeing

Compassion - the art of seeing the truth in complete acceptance of what is, awareness leading to unconditional love.

Conscience - inner state of right or wrong, the knowing voice of the soul.

Consciousness - waking, memory, thought, desires, cognition, all things in manifestation.

Consciousness thread - the bridge of light or Antahkarana, the thread that is located in the pineal gland union of life and substance.

Creative thread - the cord that links up with the center at the base of the spine. The creative thread is responsible for the development of the personality, anchored in the throat center.

Daiva - divine

Desire body - the pull of opposites.

Deva - a celestial being, shining one

Dharma - righteous conduct, life purpose or life path, God given talent.

Dhyana - fixed god realization, meditation.

Discrimination - viveka, the ability to distinguish between the real and unreal, eternal and transient, as in the upanishad maxim, "it is not this, it is not that."

Duality - the phenomenal world, where each thing exists along with its opposite; joy and sorrow etc.

Ego - individual identity

Emotional body - moving field of energy eighteen to forty-eight inches into the aura, colors, shapes and reflections of feelings.

Endurance - tolerance

Energy being - physical, etheric, emotional, mental, intuitional and divine planes of consciousness, held together by the vital force.

Equanimity - the state of remaining calm and centered throughout all changes.

Essence - the ultimate unchanging nature of things.

Etheric body - electromagnetic field surrounding the physical, circulating prana, life energy throughout the system, the protective web.

Ganesha - the elephant god that removes obstacles.

Gayatri - one of the most sacred vedic chants, goddess.

God realization - the direct and personal experience of the divine within oneself.

Grace - beloved, giving, revelation, awakening to one's true nature.

Heart chakra - the center for direct perception.

Ida - the nadi or energy channel that is left of the sushumna: intuitive, holistic, inner directed, emotional subjective, feminine, cool.

Impressions - see Samskaras or Skandas

Instinctive mind - the lower mind, which controls thought and emotion based on survival and protection.

Intellectual mind - the source of discrimination, discernment and higher perception.

Intuitional body - the vibration of our truest essence; the vehicle of the self to express, love, wisdom and truth. The holding place of akashic records, the records of the soul.

Invocation - using prayer, mantras and sound to invoke the assistance of a higher nature. The skillful knowledge of the use of energies to guide, protect and heal.

Jai - victory

Jiva - the principle of life, the individual.

Jnana - knowledge or wisdom

Jnana mudra - wisdom and preference hand gesture.

Jyoti - light

Kala - a ray, digit of manifestation the transcendental wave.

Kama - desire

Kama-manasic - the web of mind and emotions.

Karana - the prime cause.

Karma - action, the law of action and reaction, death and rebirth. We are actors in the world and reap the fruits of action, actions leave impressions, give rise to thoughts, affect our decisions, leading to further actions and impressions. The wheel of cause and effect and suffering.

Karma yoga - literally, the yoga of action.

Krishna - the name of one of the greatest teachers of India, an avatara.

Kundalini - meaning to coil, the energy that is dormant located in the root or base chakra. The home of Shakti, our pure energetic potential as human beings.

Kyan Yin - the Chinese goddess of mercy called the divine voice.

Laksmi - prosperity, success, goddess of fortune and beauty.

Lam - the seed mantra of the muladhara chakra.

Laya - absorption - whose goal is merging the individual consciousness with the divine consciousness.

Life thread - located in the heart, links the subtle bodies with a sacred grounding cord, unifying all energies. The path in which the personality unites with its divine reality. The channel for the path of return - through the form upward.

Light - clear white light, permeating all of existence, glowing, radiant, healing force of love.

Lotus petals - the Sanskrit letters inscribed on their specified number of petals indicate sound vibrations representing the varying intensities of the energies working in the different chakras.

Maha - great

Mahatma - literally the great self, a great soul.

Mala - a string of 108 beads, it is a powerful tool to help focus the mind for meditation.

Manas - mind

Manasic - the mental principle

Manipura chakra - the third chakra, located in the navel.

Mantra - a prayer, poetic hymn, incantation, sacred sound that has the power of Shakti, reflection of the ultimate and provides protection for the transmigratory life.

Maya - literally that which my be measured, that which is subject to change, illusion.

Mental body - Higher - the plane of intuition, intellect, perception, emotional intelligence, witness consciousness. Lower - The plane of reason, logic, thought, desire, amkara "I" self.

Meridian - the channels which carry prana or chi to the organs, nerves and blood vessels of the body.

Mind - Lower mind - the container of impressions that have resulted in past experiences, habits, tendencies, beliefs and memories. Higher mind - the reflection of pure consciousness, discernment, will power, discrimination. Peace of mind is the release of scars and the habits of scarring, through returning to the source from which it came. Conscious mind - wakeful, thinking state. Subconscious mind - beneath the surface, the storehouse of impressions. Super-conscious mind - the mind of light, the all knowing intelligence of the soul.

Moksha - freedom, liberation

Mudra - a mystic sign or symbol, hand gestures to seal the union of prana-apana.

Muladhara - the root chakra.

Muladhara chakra - the first or lowest center of spiritual energy located at the base of the spine.

Nada - mystical sound or energy wave.

Nadi - astral nerve or conduit. There are over 72,000 nadis in the body.

Nadis - the channels of the subtle body through which the vital, pranic and astral currents flow.

Namaskara - palms together at the heart or head area in reverence of blessings.

Namaste - "I salute the divinity within you."

Negative spiral - the soul plummets downward into negative entanglement through identification with wrong impressions.

Nirvana - the state of absolute consciousness.

Om - Sanskrit, aum

Om Mane Padme Hum - the jewel in the lotus.

Padma - lotus

Para - highest, para - unmanifested sound, the highest stage of consciousness.

Parabrahman - the absolute, eternal, boundless, immutable principle.

Parama - the most distant, hence the supreme.

Paramita - a virtue, or perfection.

Parashakti - the highest energy, the supreme goddess, the great force, primal source, all pervasive light, pure consciousness, all knowing, merging identification.

Path - a way, the way to ultimate realization, all paths lead to the same destination, uniting with source from which we have all come. Truth is one, paths are many.

Pingala - the right side of the sushumna channel. Its nature is aggressive, logical, analytical, outer directed, rational, objective, hot, masculine, mathematical and verbal.

Plane - a stage of existence.

Positive Spiral - soul ascends upward through remembering of origin.

Prana - the vital force; seat of prana is in the heart.

Pranayama - control of prana.

Purusha - the supreme being, the spirit who dwells within the body, the transcendent self.

Raja yoga - literally union with one's higher self, increasing power of discernment, selecting positive impressions which lead to higher emotions, clear and peaceful thoughts. Living in harmlessness, no sorrow for self or others.

Ram - the seed symbol of the manipura chakra.

Reincarnation - the results of karma, the birth into a physical body for the purpose of evolving love.

Repose - to rest in your true nature, resting peacefully in just being.

Rudra knot - psychic blockage in the ajna chakra, cleared by attaining the non-dual state.

Rupa - form

Sabda - sound

Sadhana - spiritual practice

Sahasrara - the seventh or highest chakra, thousand petaled lotus. The highest psychic center wherein the yogi attains union between the individual soul and the universal soul.

Samadhi - the super conscious state.

Samsara - continuous round, or wheel of births and deaths, a succession of states.

Samskaras - subtle impressions of past lives, accumulations, karmic consequences.

Sat - the one ever-present reality in the infinite world - chi - knowledge - ananda - bliss.

Satchidananda - existence, absolute knowledge, bliss.

Sattva - the quality of lightness and purity.

Satyam - truthfulness

Self realization - realization of souls actions and reactions.

Shakti - power

Shakti chalini - exercise for raising Kundalini.

Shamballa - attainment of happiness.

Shiva - the name of the third aspect of the trinity, the destroyer of evil, the regenerator.

Silver cord - this sacred cord unifies the subtle bodies and is anchored in the heart center. Through the silver cord we remain in contact with our soul.

Skandas - attributes, consciousness, form, sensation, perception, mental impressions and tendencies.

Soma - divine nectar

Soma chakra - between third eye and crown chakra.

Sorrow or suffering - self abuse

Soul - the real being of man, the relationship between spirit and matter, pure consciousness. The link between God and form, integration between spirit and matter, Christ principle, indwelling life, conscious response to matter, light between opposites.

Soul gates - knots of un-transformed consciousness, clockwise upward pull, counterclockwise gravity pull.

Spirit - illumination, enfolding, uplifting beauty.

Sristi - creation

Subconscious mind - part of the mind that is beneath the conscious mind, the impression mind. The subconscious mind is the recorder of all experiences, holder of past impressions, reactions, desires, unconscious emotions.

Subtle body - energies, which surround the physical, that extends out to higher and higher frequencies.

Suksma - the subtle body in which the different psychic centers are located.

Super consciousness - mind of light - intelligence or soul, causal mind being the cause not the effect. Universal - non-dual. Turiya - fourth state - intuitive, benevolence, universal truth.

Sushumna - the central nadi, or astral nerve, which runs through the spinal cord. The father or will aspect of our being, channels the soul energy.

Sushumna - the spiral nerve, which connects the heart with the crown center.

Sutra - the thread on which jewels are strung.

Sutratma - the thread of the self, the immortal principle of man, which incarnates from lifetime to lifetime, individuality in which countless personalities are strung. The central channel along the spine in which the free flow of energies travel on the path of return.

Swadhisthana chakra - second, or navel energy center.

Tat - "that", boundless, para brahman.

The path - the movement in consciousness to the realization of our true nature of divinity. The path takes us from identification with dense form to the formlessness of our infinite potential of beauty and freedom.

The self - the source in which "I" has sprung.

Thought forms - they arise from the deep impressions of the soul, creating disharmony or peacefulness depending on the actions or experience from the past. Thoughts are seeds of actions and experience. Pure experiences plant seeds of goodness, which is nurtured by the desire for peace, knowledge, contentment, love, power and joy, creating a foundation for peaceful thoughts.

Transcendental - the quality of being that transcends the limitations of the mind

Turiya - the state wherein the yogi sees God everywhere. The state of super consciousness. The fourth state transcending the waking dreaming and deep sleep states.

Upanishad - esoteric doctrine of the Vedas.

Vam - the seed mantra of the svadhisthana chakra.

Vasanas - subconscious inclinations, habits, patterns, impressions that are the driving force behind actions.

Vedanta - the end of all knowledge. Sri Sankaracharya is regarded as the founder of Vedanta.

Vedas - the most ancient and sacred of the Sanskrit works.

Vichar - right inquiry, the second state of jnana (knowledge).

Vidhya - knowledge

Vishnu - the second person of the Hindu trilogy, the sustaining force of the universe, the presence.

Vishnu knot - the psychic block associated with the fourth chakra anahata.

Visuddha - fifth chakra or throat energy center.

Viveka - discrimination between what is permanent and impermanent.

Vyana - the vital air or breath that governs the circulation of the body.

Will - putting into practice, ideals for well-being, activity that is harmless, not affected by past scars.

Yam - seed mantra for the anahata chakra.

Yoga - union, to join or unite.

BIBLIOGRAPHY AND
RECOMMENDED READING

Anodea, Judith. *Wheels of Life.* 1987, Llewellyn Publications, St. Paul, MN.

Bailey, A. A. *Esoteric Psychology.* vol. I, 1936. Reprint. Lucis Publishing Company, New York, 1975.

Bailey, A. A. *Esoteric Psychology.* vol. 2, 1942. Reprint. Lucis Publishing Company, New York, 1975.

Bailey, A. A. *A Treatise on Cosmic Fire.* 1925. Reprint. Lucis Publishing Company, New York, 1974.

Bailey, A. A. *A Treatise on White Magic.* 1934. Reprint. Lucis Publishing Company, New York, 1974.

Bailey, A. A. *Esoteric Healing.* 1953. Reprint. Lucis Publishing Company, New York, 1977.

Blavastsky, H.P. *The Secret Doctrine.* 1988. Reprint. Theosophical University Press, Pasadena CA, 1977.

Brennon, Barbara Ann. *Hands of Light: A Guide to Healing Through the Human Energy Field.* New York, Bantam 1993.

Brother, David Steindl-Rast. *Gratefulness, the heart of prayer - an approach to life in fullness.* 1984, Paulist Press, Ramsey NJ.

Bruyere, Rosalyn L. *Wheels of Light - A Study of the Chakras.* Fireside. Simon and Shuster, 1994.

Choa Kok Sui. *Miracles through Pranic Healing.* 1996 Sterling Publishers, Ltd. New Delhi, India.

Choa Kok Sui. *Pranic Psychotherapy.* 1989, Sterling Publishers, New Delhi.

Clifford, Terry. *Tibetan Buddhist Medicine.* 1984 Samuel Weiser.

Davis, Patricia. *Subtle Aromatherapy.* 1991, The DW Daniel Company Limited, Great Britain.

Dossey, Larrry. *Healing Words.* San Francisco, Harper Collins, 1993.

Eden, Donna. *Energy Medicine.* 1998, Tarcher/Putnam, New York.

Epstein, Gerald. *Healing Visualizations: Creating Health Through Imagery.* New York, Bantam Books 1989.

Gerber, Richard MD. 1988, *Vibrational Medicine.* Bear & Company, Santa Fe, NM.

Gerber, Richard MD. *Vibrational Medicine for the 21st Century.* Harper Collins, Publisher New York, New York.

Hodson, G. *The Seven Human Temperaments.* 1952. Reprint. Theosophical Publishing House, Adyar, India, 1981.

Hunt Roland. *The Seven Keys to Color Healing.* 1971, Harper and Row, New York, New York.

Jagadish. *Natures Way, A complete guide to health through yoga and herbal remedies.* 1999 Times Book International, Singapore.

Jurriannse, Aart. *Bridges.* 1985, Sun Center, Cape South Africa.

Kilner, Walter. *The Human Aura.* 1965 University Books, Inc.

Krishnamurti, J. *The Book of Life. Daily meditations with Krishnamurti.* 1995, Harper Collins, New York, New York.

Lama Surya Das. *Awakening the Buddha Within.* 1997, Broadway Books, New York, New York.

Lansdowne, Z. *The Rays and Esoteric Psychology.* 1989. Samuel Weiser, Inc., Box 612, York Beach, ME 03910.

Leadbeater, C. W. *The Chakras.* 1987. Reprint. Theosophical Publishing House, Wheaton, IL 60187.

Leadbeater, C. W. *Man Visible and Invisible.* Quest Books.

Lewis, Den. *The Tao of Natural Breathing.* 1998, Full Circle Publishers, Delhi, India.

Mookerjari, Ajit. *Kundalini Arousal of Inner Energy.* 1982 Thames and Hudson, LTD, London.

Motoyama, Hiroshi. *Theories of the Chakras.* 1981, Quest Books.

Myss, Caroline. *Anatomy of the Spirit.* 1996 Crown Publishers.

Natarajan, A.R. *A Practical Guide to Know Yourself, Conversations with Ramana Maharshi.* 1993 The Ramana Maharshi Center, Bangelore India.

Nisargaddatta Maharaj. *Consciousness and the Absolute - The final talks of Sri Nisargadatta Maharaj.* Edited by Jean Dunn, 1994, The Acorn Press, PO Box 3279 Durham, NC 27715-3279.

Pandit, M.P. *Kundalini Yoga.* Lotus Light Productions, Twin Lakes, WI.

Powell, A.E. *The Causal Body.* 1972. Reprint. The Theosophical Publishing House LTD, 68 Great Russell Street, London, WCIB3B.

Powell, A.E. *The Etheric Double.* 1983. Reprint. Theosophical Publishing House Ltd., London.

Powell, A.E. *The Mental Body.* 1986. Whitefriars Press, LTD. London.

Powell, A.E. *The Astral Body*. 1987. Reprint. Theosophical Publishing House, Wheaton, IL 60187.

Pundit, M. P. *Kundalini Yoga*. 1993 All India Press, Pondicherry.

Sarada, Jaya. *Trust in Yourself - Messages from the Divine*. 1988, Grace Publishing.

Saraydarian, T. *The Psyche and Psychism*. Vol 1 & 2. 1981. The Aquarian Educational Group, P.O. Box 267 Sedona AZ.

Simpson, Liz. *The Book of Chakra Healing*. 1999 Sterling Publishing Company, New York, New York.

Sree Chakravarti. *A Healers Journey*. 1993, Rudra Press, Portland, OR.

Swami Rama. Rudolf Balantine, Alan Hymes, MD *The Science of Breath*. 1979 The Himalayan International Institute, Honesdale, Pennsylvania.

Swami Sada Shiva Tirtha. *The Ayurveda Encyclopedia*. 1998, Sri Satguru Publications.

Swami Sivananda Radha. *Mantras, Words of Power*. 1980, Sterling Publishers, PVT. LTD.

Swami Sivananda. *The Science of Pranayama*. Divine Life Society, Himalayas India.

Swami Venkatesananda. *The Concise Yoga Vasistha*. State University of New York Press, Albany New York 1984.

Tansley, D. *Chakras - Rays and Radionics*. The C.W. Daniel Company Limited, Essex, England. 1984.

Tansley, David. *Radionics and the Subtle Anatomy of Man*. 1971, Great Britain, Whitstable Litho LTD, Whitstable, Kent, England.

Tansley, David. S*ubtle Bodies, Essence and Shadow*. 1985, Thames and Hudson, Great Britain.

Tansley, David. *The Raiment of Light, A study of the human aura*. 1984.
Thich Nhat Hanh. *The Heart of the Buddhas Teaching*. 1988, Parallax Press, Berkeley, California.

Willis, Pauline. *Color Therapy*. 1993 Element Books Limited, Shaftesbury, Dorset England, SP78BP.

Wood, E. *The Seven Rays*. 1985. Reprint. Theosophical Publishing House, Wheaton, IL 1984.

Worwood, Valerie Ann. *The Fragrant Mind-Aromatherapy for Personality, Mind, Mood and Emotions*. New World Library, Novato, California 1996.

Zinn, Jon Kabat. *Wherever you go there you are, mindfulness meditations in everyday life*. 1994, Hyperion 114 Fifth Avenue, New York, New York 10001.

INDEX

A

Affirmations 137, 184
Air 143
Ajna 40
Alignment 23, 36, 77, 78, 86, 99, 102, 104
Anahata 167
Astral body 6, 14, 36, 45, 46, 87, 97, 169
Atmic Plane 9
Aum 183
Aura 21, 33

B

Bridge of light 36, 137, 167, 172
Buddha 138, 211
Buddhic 9, 11, 13, 56, 70, 179

C

Causal body 9, 61, 65, 67, 70
Celestial plane 1, 69
Chakra of miracles 40, 179
Chakras 23, 39, 41, 135, 149
Christ 40, 46, 168
Conscious awakening 36
Consciousness 169, 174
Cosmic unity 42
Crown center 206, 207

D

Desire body 46
Divine affirmation 186, 188
Divine self 16

E

Earth 143
Earth element 39
Eightfold Path 211
Emotional body 34, 78, 86
Emotional plane 8, 36
Energy pathways 122

ABOUT THE AUTHOR

Jaya Sarada has dedicated her life to the search for truth. Her pursuit has led her to studies of the teachings of the masters, Theosophy and Transpersonal Psychology, in which she holds a master's degree. Jaya has traveled extensively in India to deepen her understanding of spiritual healing and is currently working on her Ph.D. in Transpersonal Counseling.

In her private practice, Jaya has developed innovative techniques for identifying areas of constricted energy and corresponding methods of release. She teaches many of these in her Parashakti Alignment Process seminars. *The Path of Return,* the first of a trilogy of healing works intended as texts to accompany her teaching, shares many of those techniques. Jaya is also the author of *Trust in Yourself - Messages from the Divine.*

The founder of Grace Foundation, Jaya lives on Whidbey Island in Washington state with her partner Thomas, and her daughter Arielle.

For more information about Jaya Sarada and Grace Foundation please visit www.gracefoundation.org or e-mail Jaya at gracepublishing@aol.com.

ABOUT THE ARTIST

The art on the cover of this book, the mandalas and the images on pages 43, 134 and 216 are the work of Templeton, California artist Karen Foster Wells.

For information about Foster Wells and her work contact Grace Foundation 1-800-282-5292

SEMINARS

Jaya Sarada is available for private training, as well as group sessions for corporations, schools and other organizations.

The Parashakti Alignment Process
   The beginning course will teach you how to open channels for the healing light and create optimal spiritual understanding.

Soul Development and Intuitive Counseling Training
   This class assists you in evolving to your true nature and potential. Exercises in journal writing, meditation, visualization, prayer and connecting with your spirit guide will be shared.

AuraTouch™
   Using your hands to scan, balance and bring light and energy into the aura. Offered as a weekend or series.

Chakra Healing
   Learn about the energy centers of the body, mind and emotions and balance them through spiritual transformation.

Energy Testing and Pendulum Work
   Learn the art of muscle testing and the use of pendulums to dialogue with the body, mind and soul.

The Path of the Sacred
   An opportunity to explore ways of reconnecting with your divine origin through meditation, chanting, mantras, journal writing and more. Based on the upcoming book.

The Path of Return - A Gathering in Conscious Awareness
   Return to the source of your consciousness through understanding your energy system, a pathway to your soul. Map the energy system. Receive light and guidance to your true nature.

Shakti Source Points, A meditative acupressure technique
   Learn the ancient art of point work with an emphasis on breathing and meditation.

Please call Grace Foundation for more information.
1-800-282-5292

ORDER FORM

Qty.	Item	Price	S&H	Total
	Books by Jaya Sarada:			
	Trust in Yourself - Messages from the Divine	**13.95**	4.75	
	The Path of Return - The Light of Parashakti	**16.95**	4.75	
	(Books available wholesale in quantities of ten or more, please call for additional information)			
	Set of 15 Colored Charts (Seven chakras, energy anatomy and planes of consciousness)	**30.00**	6.50	
			Sub Total	
		Shipping and Handling Total		
			Tax	
			Order Total	

Method of Payment:
AE   VISA   MC   Discover   Check_____

CC#_____ Expiration_____

Name:_____
Name as it appears on the credit card

Shipping Address:_____

City, State, Zip_____

Phone: (_____)_____-_____

Guided meditations and books on tape by Jaya Sarada, pendulums, Sacred Space Creation are available through our on-line catalog at www.gracefoundation.com.
Please contact Customer Service at 1-800-282-5292 to confirm order or e-mail your order to graceorders@aol.com.